### Frugal Food is a temporary solution for tough times

Many of us have been through tough times and wished we were able to navigate those times a little more easily. A friend shared how she dealt with feeding her boys, when all she had was a few pieces of bread, Vegemite and not enough cheese for everyone. The result was Tiger Toast for dinner – fun, creative and frugal.

**Frugal Food** will provide you with more than Tiger Toast for a meal!

Being frugal to get through tough times may mean menu planning, cooking ahead, freezing food, cheaper cuts of meats, more lentils and sticking to the budget.

**Frugal Food** can help you in the short term to navigate those tough times. It has a variety of foods, interesting meals and easy-preparation recipes. Plus, all meals and shopping lists are planned out for you. No added stress, we have done all the planning for you to just follow.

**Frugal Food** will help if you are:

- a single-income household
- time-poor and trying to juggle after-school activities
- a single parent trying to make ends meet
- saving for a special holiday or house deposit
- recently unemployed.

Perhaps you just want to save money and reduce food waste, or you're not great at planning the family's menus and shopping lists for the week.

**Frugal Food** provides:

- full menu plans for the week, including all meals and some snacks
- a complete shopping list for each fortnight to feed a family of four
- easy-to-follow recipes.

Until you try it, you won't believe:

- how much money you will save
- how much extra time you will have because the planning is done for you
- how easy your shopping will be, having a prepared list.

We faced some challenging times when we had to tighten our belts to make sure we could feed our families and put a roof over their heads, all on a minimal budget.

So, we became frugal and developed and used these menus, lists and recipes for our families. It made planning, shopping and cooking the easiest it had ever been, and we saved money and time. Being frugal during tough times helped us to get back on our feet. When we had more in the budget, we were able to add more fruit, vegetables or salad to the meals and portion sizes could be larger.

Overall, being frugal during tough times and then continuing to follow a budget allowed us to go on family outings and holidays, and create cherished memories that will last a lifetime.

We hope this book gives you the chance to save money, enjoy meals together, and allows you to get through tough times and create some special memories with your family.

*Love, Kate and Andrea*

Copyright © Andrea Miller and Kate Smith 2021, 2024

The moral right of the authors has been asserted.

Second Revised Edition 2024

First published in Australia in 2021 by
Frugal Food,
PO Box 59, Strathpine,
Queensland, Australia.

frugalfoodlife@outlook.com

ISBN 978-0-646-89181-1

All rights reserved. No part of this book may be reproduced or transmitted by any person or entity (including Google, Amazon, or similar organisation), in any form or by any means, electronic or mechanical, including photocopying, recording, scanning or by any information storage and retrieval system, without prior permission in writing from the publisher.

A catalogue record for this book is available from the National Library of Australia

**10% of profits go to Broken to Brilliant, a charity supporting domestic violence survivors.**

## Contents

### Fortnight 1
Menu ........................... 4
Shopping List ............ 5
Tips for fortnight ...... 6
Recipes ....................... 7

### Fortnight 2
Menu ......................... 14
Shopping List ......... 15
Tips for fortnight ... 16
Recipes .................... 17

### Fortnight 3
Menu ......................... 22
Shopping List ......... 23
Tips for fortnight ... 24
Recipes .................... 25

### Fortnight 4 – Vegetarian
Menu ......................... 30
Shopping List ......... 31
Tips for fortnight ... 32
Recipes .................... 33

### Abbreviations
tsp = teaspoon (5 ml)
tbs = tablespoon (20 ml)
g = gram
kg = kilogram
ml = millilitre

### Tasted, tried and tested stories for Frugal Food

"I'd like to say a huge thank you for the *Frugal Food* menus, food plan and shopping list. I find it hard to find nutritious ways to feed my family, especially when my budget is so tight.

"With the recipes on hand I was able to feed my family without the stress of hunting for a recipe and overpaying for ingredients that I will never use again. My family is happy, enjoying the variety of delicious food and I'm definitely loving it. This has really opened my eyes into a world of value cooking, and I could not be more grateful to have this little power tool in my kitchen.

"10/10 would recommend."

**Jess, Brisbane, Queensland**

## About the Authors

**Andrea Miller** has not only been a professional ballet dancer, fitness instructor, business trainer, charity director and author, but has also had 22 years in the health care industry and been tight for cash as a single mother.

**Kate Smith** is a mum of two who has had to scrape through during tough times and feed her family on a budget. Kate grew up with cooking featuring strongly in her life, helping in the kitchen cooking for the family from an early age, studying cooking, and working in the food industry before moving into the field of health, nursing, health promotion and domestic violence responses.

## Tips for frugal cooking and time saving

### Frugal cooking means:

- taking a few minutes to check what's ahead in this fortnight
- undertaking bulk preparation of certain foods
- being aware of portion control
- buying no-name brands and in-season fruit
- using cost-effective alternative items such as lentils to add extra protein to a meal.

### It will help to:

- Cut cheese into blocks so it is allocated ready for each meal.
- Soak the chickpeas and lentils overnight so they won't need to be cooked for so long. Then cook and cool, divide into bags, and freeze.
- Divide meat and chicken into individual portions ready for each meal. It is so much easier to defrost what you need, and saves time when you are cooking meals.
- Freeze any leftovers, as you never know when you might want a cooking-free night.
- If possible, purchase the bread and/or milk you need daily, as some of the big supermarkets have a free piece of fruit for children when they are in store.
- Look to purchase items on special that are cheaper than your shopping list, as this can save you additional money.

### If there is additional money in the budget:

- Swap white bread for wholemeal or wholegrain bread, or wholegrain sourdough.
- Purchase ham to add to quiche or sandwiches.
- Always add more fruit and vegetables when you can afford them, with the aim of eating 2 serves of fruit and 5 or more serves of vegetables each day per person.
- Choose a variety of colours of fresh vegetables and fruits – green, orange, red, yellow, purple and white.
- When purchasing a treat, try to get one that also has some nutritional value, such as yoghurt, berries, nuts or muesli bars.

## How to use Frugal Food menus, shopping lists and food plans

**1.** Have a quick look over the full menu for the fortnight and get excited about having a different meal every night!

**2.** Read the fortnightly tips page before you go shopping, so you have an idea how it would be best for you to handle the bread and milk you need for the fortnight.

**3.** Take a photo on your phone or print a copy of the shopping list, so you don't miss anything when you do the fortnight's shopping.

**4.** Everything you need for the fortnight is on that shopping list. There will be some items you purchase in the first or second fortnights that will last for following weeks, and you'll still have some left, such as spices.

**5.** When you come home from shopping refer to the fortnightly tips page, and allow 15 minutes to divide up your meats and cheeses into portion sizes.

**6.** Simply follow the menu plan for each day, trying to keep the days in order if possible.

# MENU: Fortnight 1

| Week 1 | SUN | MON | TUES | WED | THURS | FRI | SAT |
|---|---|---|---|---|---|---|---|
| **Breakfast** | Wheat breakfast biscuit /Porridge/ Pancakes | Wheat breakfast biscuit /Porridge/ Pancakes | Wheat breakfast biscuit /Porridge/ Pancakes | Wheat breakfast biscuit /Porridge/ Pancakes | Wheat breakfast biscuit /Porridge/ Pancakes | Wheat breakfast biscuit /Porridge/ Pancakes | Wheat breakfast biscuit /Porridge/ Pancakes / Egg on toast |
| **Morning tea** | Home-baked biscuits Fruit in season | Home-baked biscuits Fruit in season | Home-baked biscuits Fruit in season | Home-baked biscuits Fruit in season | Home-baked biscuits Fruit in season | Home-baked biscuits Fruit in season | Home-baked biscuits Fruit in season |
| **Lunch** | Rice and Vegie Pie | Chicken sandwiches | Chicken and carrot sandwiches | Tomato sandwiches | Egg and carrot sandwiches | Cheese sandwiches | Leftover lunch |
| **Afternoon tea** | Home-baked biscuits Half an apple cut into pieces and carrot sticks | Home-baked biscuits Half an apple cut into pieces and carrot sticks | Home-baked biscuits Half an apple cut into pieces and carrot sticks | Home-baked biscuits Half an apple cut into pieces and carrot sticks | Home-baked biscuits Half an apple cut into pieces and carrot sticks | Home-baked biscuits Half an apple cut into pieces and carrot sticks | Home-baked biscuits Fruit in season |
| **Dinner** | Slow Cooked Chicken and Rice (save leftover stock) | Zucchini and Chicken Slice | Spinach and Ricotta Cannelloni | Quick Quiche | TexMex Rice | Stir Fried Mince and Rice | Lentil and Vegie Patties |
| **Dessert** | Apple Cake and custard | Apple Cake and custard | | Apple crumble | Apple crumble | | Pancakes |

| Week 2 | SUN | MON | TUES | WED | THURS | FRI | SAT |
|---|---|---|---|---|---|---|---|
| **Breakfast** | Wheat breakfast biscuit /Porridge/ Pancakes | Wheat breakfast biscuit /Porridge/ Pancakes | Wheat breakfast biscuit /Porridge/ Pancakes | Wheat breakfast biscuit /Porridge/ Pancakes | Wheat breakfast biscuit /Porridge/ Pancakes | Wheat breakfast biscuit /Porridge/ Pancakes | Wheat breakfast biscuit /Porridge/ Pancakes / Egg on toast |
| **Morning tea** | Home-baked biscuits Fruit in season | Fruit in season Oat biscuits | Fruit in season Oat biscuits | Fruit in season Apple Cake | Fruit in season Apple Cake | Home-baked biscuits Fruit in season | Home-baked biscuits Fruit in season |
| **Lunch** | Rice and Vegie Pie | Egg sandwiches | Tomato and leftover mince sandwiches | Tomato sandwiches | Egg sandwiches | Egg sandwiches | Leftover lunch |
| **Afternoon tea** | Home-baked biscuits Fruit in season | Home-baked biscuits Fruit in season | Home-baked biscuits Fruit in season | Home-baked biscuits Fruit in season | Hummus and flatbread Fruit in season | Hummus and flatbread Fruit in season | Hummus on Wheat breakfast biscuit Fruit in season |
| **Dinner** | Zucchini and Carrot Savoury Slice | Mince, Lentil and Spinach Curry | Echidnas | Beef and Lentil Pasta | Corn Fritters | Vegie Fried Rice | Boiled egg and toast |
| **Dessert** | Apple crumble | Apple crumble | | Apple and custard | Apple and custard | | |

# SHOPPING LIST: Fortnight 1

| QTY | Product | Check |
|---|---|---|
| 1 | Bicarbonate of Soda 500 g | |
| 1 | Imitation Vanilla Essence 200 ml | |
| 1 | Freezer Bag Medium 80 pack | |
| 1 | Pasta Cannelloni 250 g | |
| 1 | Pasta Spirals 500 g | |
| 2 | Rolled Oats 1 kg | |
| 1 | Wheat Breakfast Biscuits 800 g (approx. 52 biscuits). If the larger 1 kg (approx. 66 biscuits) or 1.2 kg pack is on special, buy it. | |
| 1 | Vegetable Stock Powder 168 g | |
| 1 | Nutmeg 25 g | |
| 1 | Cinnamon 25 g | |
| 1 | Taco Seasoning Mix 35 g | |
| 1 | Mild Curry Powder 50 g | |
| 2 | Diced Tomatoes 800 g | |
| 1 | Italian Passata 700 g | |
| 1 | Vegetable Oil 750 ml | |
| 1 | Chickpeas 375 g | |
| 1 | Brown Lentils 1 kg | |
| 1 | Long Grain Rice 2 kg | |
| 1 | Sweetened Condensed Milk 397 g | |
| 1 | Condensed Tomato Soup Can 420 g | |
| 1 | Baking Powder 125 g | |
| 1 | White Plain Flour 2 kg | |
| 1 | Sugar 2 kg | |
| 1 | Desiccated Coconut 500 g | |
| 1 | Custard Powder 350 g | |
| 1 | Creamed Corn 420 g | |
| 1 | Corn Kernels 420 g | |
| 1 | Soy Sauce 500 ml | |
| 1 | White Vinegar 2 L | |
| 4 | Apple Pie Slices, canned 410 g | |
| | **Fruit and Vegetables** | |
| 2 | Carrots prepacked 1.5 kg | |
| 1 | Onions prepacked 1 kg | |
| 3 | Green zucchini approx. 150 g | |
| 1 | Tomatoes prepacked 1 kg (approx. 8 tomatoes) | |
| 1 | Fresh fruit in season, e.g. pears, apples, bananas | |
| 1 | Garlic approx. 60 g | |
| 1 | Apples prepacked 1 kg | |
| 1 | Lemon | |

| QTY | Product | Check |
|---|---|---|
| | **Cold and Frozen Items** | |
| 2 | Full Cream Milk 3 L | |
| 1 | Thickened Cream 600 ml | |
| 1 | Frozen Spinach Portions 250 g | |
| 2 | Frozen Australian Carrots Peas and Corn 1 kg | |
| 1 | Australian Tasty Cheddar Cheese Block 1 kg | |
| 2 | Eggs 12 pack | |
| 1 | Whole Chicken approx. 1.8-2 kg | |
| 4 | Chicken Drumsticks | |
| 1 | Butter 500 g | |
| 1 | Smooth Ricotta 375 g | |
| 1 | Beef Mince 1 kg | |
| | **Bread** | |
| 5 | Sandwich Bread Loaf 680g (white, brown or wholegrain) | |
| 1 | Soft Wraps 8 pack | |

# TIPS FOR MANAGING THIS FORTNIGHT OF COOKING

**Reminder**: Budget cooking means bulk recipes, portion control and using less expensive items such as lentils to add the protein to a meal but at a much cheaper cost than meat. It also means you need to get ready with food preparation.

Get ready for this fortnight:

- Cut up cheese into 6 even blocks so it is allocated ready for each meal.
- Soak the chickpeas overnight; keep the bag for cooking instructions. Cook and cool and divide the chickpeas into 1-cup bags. Place half the bags in the fridge and the other half in the freezer.
- Soak the brown lentils overnight; keep the bag for cooking instructions. Top up with water in the morning. Cook and cool and divide cooked lentils into 1-cup bags. Place half in the fridge and the other half in the freezer.
- Freeze 4 loaves of bread (or put aside the money to buy fresh when needed).
- Divide up the mince into:
  » 1 x 200 g bag labelled for the Stir-Fried Mince
  » 1 x 200 g bag labelled for Mince, Lentil and Spinach Curry
  » 1 x 200 g bag labelled for the Beef and Lentil Pasta
  » 1 x 200 g bag labelled for the Rice and Mince
  » 1 x 200 g bag labelled for Echidnas.
- Take the spinach out of the freezer the morning of cooking the Spinach Cannelloni.
- Use only 3 eggs for the sandwiches as the carrot and mayonnaise make it go further.
- I was able to make 5 sandwiches from the chicken and egg sandwiches. Your choice: add the extra quarter sandwich to lunchboxes for morning tea, or put in the freezer for a snack later in the fortnight.
- Freeze any leftovers to have for cooking-free meals.

**IF THERE IS ADDITIONAL MONEY IN THE BUDGET:**

- Swap white bread for wholemeal or wholegrain bread, or wholegrain sourdough.
- Purchase ham to add to the quiche or for sandwiches.
- Always add more fruit and vegetables as you can afford them, with the aim of eating 2 serves of fruit and more than 5 serves of vegetables each day per person.
- Purchase olive oil instead of vegetable or sunflower oil.

(Image © Kate Crowley Smith)

# RECIPES: Fortnight 1

## Porridge

2 cups/180 g rolled oats (preferably wholemeal)
2 ½ cups/600 ml milk
pinch of salt

1. Place the oats and the milk in a large saucepan over medium heat.
2. Add a tiny pinch of salt and use a wooden spoon to stir.
3. Slowly bring to a simmer for 5 to 6 minutes, stirring as often as you can to give you a smooth, creamy porridge.
4. For a thinner porridge, add more milk until you get the consistency you like.
5. This can be made in a small slow cooker overnight.
6. Top with canned pie apples for sweetness or fresh fruit and nuts if desired.

## Pancakes/Pikelets

1 ½ cups milk
1 egg
2 tsp vanilla essence
2 cups self-raising flour (make from plain flour by adding 2 tsp baking powder per 1 cup of plain flour)
¼ tsp bicarbonate of soda
⅓ cup caster sugar
25 g butter, melted

1. Whisk milk, egg and vanilla together in a jug. Sift flour and bicarbonate of soda into a bowl. Stir in sugar. Make a well in the centre. Add milk mixture. Whisk until just combined.
2. Heat a large non-stick frying pan over medium heat. Brush pan with butter. Using ¼ cup mixture per pancake, cook pancakes for 3 to 4 minutes or until bubbles appear on the surface. Turn and cook for a further 3 minutes or until cooked through.

*Slow Cooked Chicken (Image © Kate Crowley Smith)*

## Slow Cooked Chicken

1 whole chicken
4 chicken drumsticks
1 onion, quartered
2 cloves garlic, quartered
2 large or 4 small carrots, cut into large pieces
pepper and salt
2 tbs soy sauce
8-10 cups of water – the water needs to cover the chicken
1 tsp of stock powder per cup of water

1. Place chicken in a slow cooker. Add onion, garlic, carrots, salt, pepper and soy sauce and cover with water. Cover and cook 4 hours on high or 8 hours on a low setting. Remove chicken from stock and use for other recipes (sandwiches, Chicken and Rice, and Zucchini and Chicken Slice).
2. Strain vegetables from stock and keep. Freeze the stock and a small amount of chicken for the end of the week.

### TIPS

Keep the carrot, onion, garlic, and vegies from the stock, mash and freeze. Use these in the lentil patties or the curry.

Stock can also be made from powdered stock and hot water, 1-2 tsp of stock powder per cup of water.

## Slow Cooked Chicken and Rice

2 cups of cooked rice (½ cup per person) flavoured with chicken/vegie stock powder
2 cups of frozen peas, corn and carrots
2 chicken drumsticks and the 2 thighs

1. Cook rice with chicken/vegie stock flavour.
2. Stir in heated mixed vegies.
3. Top each plate with one heated chicken drumstick or one thigh.

## Zucchini and Chicken Slice

1 zucchini, grated
1 onion, grated
200 g / ¾ cup grated cheese
½ cup shredded chicken
1 cup self-raising flour (make from plain flour by adding 2 tsps

*Rice and Vegie Pie, p9.* (Image © Stephanie Frey)

baking powder per 1 cup of plain flour)
50 g butter, melted
3 eggs, beaten
¼ cup milk

1. Combine grated vegies, cheese and chicken into one bowl.
2. Stir self-raising flour into vegies, cheese and chicken mix.
3. Melt butter and slowly add butter to the bowl with beaten egg and milk. Mix well.
4. Place into a greased loaf tin and cook in a moderate oven for 30-40 mins.

### TIPS
Top with tomato slices if you have some tomato spare. Serve hot or cold.

## Spinach and Ricotta Cannelloni

250 g frozen spinach, thawed
225 g fresh ricotta cheese (save the remaining cheese for the Quick Quiche)
2 egg yolks
1 clove garlic, crushed
½ cup grated cheese (plus extra for serving)
salt and pepper to taste
250 g cannelloni
700 g Italian passata sauce

1. Mix spinach, ricotta cheese, egg yolks, garlic, grated cheese, salt and pepper together thoroughly in a medium-sized bowl.
2. Fill cannelloni tubes with the prepared mixture; only fill the tubes about ¾ full.
3. Grease an ovenproof baking dish and pour a layer of passatta sauce over the base, retaining enough to cover the cannelloni.
4. Place a single layer of filled cannelloni side by side in the baking dish. Pour over the remaining sauce and sprinkle with extra grated cheese.
5. Bake in an oven at 200°C for 25-35 minutes (test by pricking with a skewer).

## Quick Quiche

### BASIC QUICHE INGREDIENTS
crust ends from the loaves of bread
4 eggs
¾ cup cream
¾ cup milk
150 g ricotta (leftover from cannelloni recipe)
200 g / ¾ cup cheese
salt and pepper to taste

### QUICHE FLAVOURS
2 chopped tomatoes
finely chopped onion (small amount)

1. Preheat oven to 180°C.
2. Roll bread with a pastry roller. Butter bread and press into muffin tins, butter side down, and bake 3-5 mins until light brown.
3. While the toasted shells are cooking, put the eggs into a bowl and briskly whisk, then add in all other ingredients and mix well.
4. When toasted shells are lightly brown, remove from oven, pour in the wet ingredients and bake for a further 15 mins, until the centre of the quiches are firm.

## TexMex Rice

1 cup long grain rice
2 cups of stock (500 ml)
1 packet of Mexican mix/Taco Seasoning Mix
400 g diced tomatoes (about 4 medium tomatoes)
400 g pre-cooked chickpeas or pre-cooked lentils
1 cup frozen carrots, peas and corn

1. Combine all ingredients except frozen vegetables and bring to the boil.
2. Cover, reduce the heat and simmer for 12 minutes or until the rice is soft. Add in frozen vegetables 5 minutes before the end. Stir occasionally.

TIPS
Use stock from slow cooked chicken, or make stock from powdered stock and water, 1-2 tsp of stock powder per cup of water.

## Stir Fried Mince and Rice

2 cups of rice
1 tbs oil
1 onion, finely chopped
1 clove garlic, finely chopped
200 g mince
1 cup frozen peas, corn and carrots
1 cup of pre-cooked lentils
soy sauce
pepper and salt to taste
1 grated carrot

1. Boil the rice until soft.
2. Heat a non-stick pan, add oil and gently fry the onion and garlic until transparent.
3. Add mince and fry until brown.
4. Add mixed frozen vegies and lentils and cook through.
5. Add soy sauce, and salt and pepper, to taste.
6. Add grated carrot and heat through.
7. Add cooked rice and stir through mince dish.

VARIATION - IF AVAILABLE FUNDS
Add coriander, chilli to taste, lime/lemon juice, bean sprouts, capsicum, or celery.

## Lentil and Vegie Patties

10 wheat breakfast biscuits, crushed
125 g pre-cooked brown lentils
125 g pre-cooked chickpeas
1 cup frozen carrots, peas and corn
1 large onion, finely chopped
2 large carrots, grated
¼ to ½ tsp curry powder to taste
salt and pepper to taste
4 eggs
2 tbs flour
a little vegetable oil for frying

1. In a large mixing bowl add half of the crushed wheat breakfast biscuits. Set the rest aside for coating the patties.
2. Add cooked lentils and chickpeas, onion, carrots, curry powder, salt and pepper to the large mixing bowl and stir well.
3. Lightly whisk 2 eggs with a fork, add to the mixture and combine thoroughly. (If the mixture is too dry add 1tbs water.)
4. In a separate bowl add some flour. This is for coating the patties.
5. Whisk the remaining eggs in a bowl and set aside.
6. Take 1 tablespoon of pattie mix and shape into a pattie, toss in the flour, then the egg mixture, making sure the egg coats the entire pattie. Then cover the pattie with the remaining crushed wheat breakfast biscuits.
7. On medium heat, shallow fry the patties in a little oil until each side is golden brown.
8. Drain the patties on paper towel to absorb any excess oil.

## Rice and Vegie Pie

1 zucchini
1 tomato
1 cup of cooked rice
1 cup frozen carrots, peas and corn
2 cups of onion and cheese sauce
¼ cup cheese

1. Dice zucchini and tomato and fry vegies, until just cooked.
2. Combine cooked rice, vegies and onion and cheese sauce.
3. Place in a casserole dish, top with extra tomato and cheese if you have some.
4. Bake in a moderate oven for 15-20 mins.

## Onion and Cheese Sauce

50 g butter
1 onion, finely diced
5 tbs plain flour
600 ml warm milk
½ cup cheese, grated
salt and pepper

1. Melt the butter in a small saucepan. Stir in the finely diced onion. Cook until the onion is transparent.
2. Stir in the flour. Cook, stirring continuously, for 1 minute, until the mixture forms a smooth 'roux'.
3. Remove the pan from the heat and gradually pour in the warm milk, stirring or whisking constantly. Return the pan to the heat and bring to the boil, still stirring or whisking.
4. Reduce the heat and simmer the white sauce gently for 2 minutes, stirring occasionally, until it is smooth and thick. Add grated cheese.

*Zucchini and Carrot Savoury Slice*
(Image © Atides)

5. Season to taste with salt and pepper.

**VARIATION - IF AVAILABLE FUNDS**
Add ½ cup cooked pumpkin and/or sweet potato.

## Zucchini and Carrot Savoury Slice

1 zucchini
1 carrot
1 onion
3 eggs
1 cup self-raising flour (make from plain flour by adding 2 tsps baking powder per 1 cup of plain flour)
200 g / ¾ cup cream
salt and pepper to taste

1. Preheat oven to 180°C.
2. Trim ends of the zucchini and grate.
3. Grate carrot and onion.
4. Beat eggs.
5. Combine all ingredients.
6. Press into a well-greased loaf tin lined with baking paper.
7. Cook for approx. 40 mins, until the centre of the slice is firm.

**VARIATION - IF AVAILABLE FUNDS**
Add ham or bacon.

## Mince, Lentil and Spinach Curry

2 tbs butter
1 onion, finely diced
2-3 cloves garlic, finely chopped
Curry powder (if you have a range of spices, use these spices instead: 2 tsp ground cumin, 2 tsp ground coriander, 2 tsp ground paprika, 1 tsp garam masala)
200 g beef mince
1 tin / 800 g diced tomatoes
1½ cups pre-cooked brown lentils
1 litre vegetable stock
1 bunch English spinach (or 250 g packet frozen spinach) or add carrots and zucchini, frozen vegies (2 cups)
fresh coriander (optional)
salt and pepper to taste
2 cups cooked rice

1. Sauté onions in 1 tbs butter until golden. Add garlic (optional ginger), stirring until softened. Add dry spices, stir through then remove.
2. In a little more butter, brown the mince, breaking it up until cooked through.
3. Return onion/spice mixture and combine.
4. Add tinned tomatoes, pre-cooked brown lentils and stock. Bring to boil, reduce heat and simmer, covered, for one hour, stirring now and then.
5. Add grated carrot and zucchini.
6. If using fresh spinach, rinse, remove stalks and shred, tossing through mince at the end of the hour. If cut finely it'll cook in the mince. If using frozen spinach, have it defrosted and ready to add at the end of the hour.
7. Season with salt and pepper and serve over cooked rice.

**TIPS**
Stock can be made from powdered stock and water, 1-2 tsp of stock powder per cup of water.

**VARIATION - IF AVAILABLE FUNDS**
If available you can add 1 finely chopped green chilli, 1 finely chopped red chilli or add some chilli powder to taste and a 2cm piece of fresh ginger, grated.

If you have extra cooked chickpeas in the freezer add these as well.

## Echidnas

200 g mince
1 finely chopped onion
1 cup pre-cooked brown lentils
½ cup uncooked rice
2 crushed wheat breakfast biscuits
salt and pepper to taste
finely chopped parsley (if

*Mince, Lentil and Spinach Curry* (Image © Kate Crowley Smith)

available in the garden)

2 tbs plain flour

1 420 g can of condensed tomato soup

2 ½ cups of water or stock

1-2 grated carrots

2 cups of frozen peas, corn and carrots

1. Combine mince, onion, cooked lentils, uncooked rice, crushed wheat breakfast biscuits, pepper and salt, parsley or dried herbs and flour.
2. Shape into balls about the size of a soup spoon.
3. In a large saucepan bring the soup and water to boil; add grated carrots.
4. Drop in the meatballs.
5. Cover and simmer for 25 mins.
6. Add frozen vegies and cook for a further 5 mins.

These are called Echidnas as the rice sticks out of the meatballs.

### TIPS

Stock can be made from powdered stock and water, 1-2 tsp of stock powder per cup of water.

## Beef and Lentil Pasta

300 g pasta
1 tbs butter
1 onion, finely chopped
1 garlic clove crushed
200 g minced beef
1-2 carrots, grated
1 cup of frozen, peas, carrots and corn
800 g tin chopped tomatoes
¾ cup stock
1 cup pre-cooked brown lentils
grated cheese to serve

1. Cook the pasta according to packet instructions or until al dente.
2. While the pasta is cooking, heat the butter in a large frying pan over medium heat and sauté the onion and garlic until fragrant. Cook for a further 2-3 minutes or until the onion is soft (mushrooms can be added here).
3. Add the beef and brown all over, separating the mince with a wooden spoon as it cooks. Add the grated carrot and frozen vegetables and cook for 2-3 minutes.
4. Add the chopped tomatoes and stock. Bring to the boil, reduce the heat and simmer, stirring occasionally, for around 15 minutes or until the liquid has reduced.
5. Add the pre-cooked lentils and parsley and cook for a further 5 minutes. Serve with the pasta and cheese.

### VARIATION - IF AVAILABLE FUNDS

Add mushrooms.

### TIPS

Stock can be made from powdered stock and water, 1-2 tsp of stock powder per cup of water.

## Corn Fritters and Tomato Salsa

½ cup plain flour
1 tsp baking powder
2 eggs
¼ cup milk (add a little more if too thick)
1 x 420 g corn kernels drained
1 x 420 g creamed corn
oil (for frying)

SALSA
1 onion (diced)
2 tomatoes (diced)

1. Mix flour, baking powder and salt into a mixing bowl.
2. Add beaten eggs, creamed

*Corn Fritters* (Image © Kate Crowley Smith)

corn and corn kernels, then milk (add a little more if too thick). Mix well.

3. Heat 1–2 tbs of oil in a non-stick frying pan. Place spoonfuls of the corn fritter mixture into the pan.
4. Cook over medium heat for 2-3 minutes.
5. Turn and cook the other side for a further 2-3 minutes until fritters are golden and cooked through. Serve with salsa.

### VARIATION - IF AVAILABLE FUNDS

To make this a little different each time or to add more flavour you can add parsley, chives, dried herbs, onion to taste, grated zucchini, capsicum, avocado or celery.

## Vegie Fried Rice

2 tsp oil
1 cup finely chopped onions
4 cloves garlic, minced
3 cups frozen vegies – carrots, peas and corn
1 cup cooked chickpeas
3 cups cooked rice*
3-4 tsp soy sauce, to taste

1. Heat oil in a large non-stick wok (or large, deep skillet) over medium-high heat. Add onions and garlic. Sauté 3 minutes. Add vegies and chickpeas and cook through.

2. Stir in cooked rice and soy sauce. Cook and toss for 2 minutes. Serve warm.

*It also works best if you can prepare the rice a day in advance.

**VARIATION - IF AVAILABLE FUNDS**

Add 2 large eggs if available. Move vegies over to one side of the pan, crack the egg into the opposite side; scramble until cooked; mix through the rice.

## Apple Cake

150 g butter, softened
1 tin apple slices
1 cup sugar
2 eggs
2 cups plain flour, sifted
5 tsp baking powder
2 tsp cinnamon

1. Preheat oven to 140°C.
2. Grease a square cake tin.
3. Combine all ingredients in a bowl and stir well. Pour into the prepared cake tin.
4. Bake in the preheated oven for 45 minutes or until cooked through.

**VARIATIONS**

Place mixture into 6 muffin tins and the rest of the mixture into a loaf tin.

Spoon a small amount of apple onto the top of the mixture in the loaf tin.

Sprinkle all cakes with cinnamon sugar – mix 1 tsp cinnamon and 1 tsp caster sugar.

## Apple Crumble

2 tbs butter
2 tins of apple slices
¼ cup packed brown sugar or caster sugar
2 tsp plain flour

**CRUMBLE TOPPING**

1 cup coconut
1 cup crushed wheat breakfast biscuits (approx. 5)
½ cup rolled oats
¼ cup caster sugar
½ cup plain flour
80 g butter

1. Preheat oven to 180°C and grease a baking dish with butter.
2. In a bowl mix the tinned apple slices, sugar and flour and pour into baking dish.
3. Place all of the topping ingredients into a bowl and mix until it starts to form clumps.
4. Once the topping mixture is thoroughly mixed, place over apple layer.

5. Bake in an oven for 30-40 mins or until golden brown.
6. Remove apple crumble from the oven and let stand for 10 mins.
7. Serve with custard.

**VARIATIONS**

Add ½ tsp of cinnamon to the crumble mix.

If you have any uneaten apples, slice finely and add these to the apple mix.

## Custard

¼ cup custard powder
2 ½ cups (625 ml) milk
2 tbs caster sugar

1. Combine custard powder and ¼ cup of the milk in a small jug. Stir until smooth.
2. Place custard mixture, sugar and remaining milk in a small saucepan over medium-low heat, stirring constantly until custard comes to the boil and thickens. Simmer, stirring for 1 minute.

## Basic Biscuit Dough

½ cup sugar
500 g butter
1 can of condensed milk
4 ½ cups plain flour
5 tsp baking powder

1. Cream the sugar and butter. Add condensed milk, flour, and baking powder.
2. Divide the biscuit dough into 4.

**PLAIN BISCUITS**

¼ of the dough can be plain biscuits.

**CUSTARD BISCUITS**

To ¼ of the dough add 3 tbs of custard powder, mix well and add single drops of milk at a time until a nice ball of dough forms.

*Apple Crumble* (Image © Svetlana Poselentseva)

*Choc chip biscuit variation*
(Image © Kate Crowley Smith)

**COCONUT BISCUITS**

To ¼ of the dough add ⅔ cup of desiccated coconut, mix well and add single drops of milk at a time until a nice ball of dough forms.

**CUSTARD, COCONUT AND OAT BISCUITS**

To ¼ of the dough add ⅓ cup coconut, ⅓ cup oats, 3 tbs of custard powder. Mix well and add single drops of milk at a time until a nice ball of dough forms.

**COOKING**

1. Place teaspoon-sized balls onto a flat oven tray. Use baking paper to prevent the biscuits sticking, or grease the tray.
2. Bake in moderate oven (approx. 180°C) for 10-15 minutes until golden brown.

**VARIATION - IF AVAILABLE FUNDS**

Add chocolate chips to any biscuits if you have some extra cash.

**EXTRA RECIPES IF ENOUGH INGREDIENTS IN THE CUPBOARD:**

## Coconut and Oat Biscuits

250 g butter
¾ cup brown sugar (substitute white sugar if you do not have this)
¾ cup white/caster sugar
2 eggs
1 tsp vanilla essence (if not available, leave out)
2 cups self-raising flour
2 cups rolled oats
1 cup desiccated coconut

1. Preheat oven to 180°C.
2. In a medium mixing bowl cream butter and sugars. Add egg and vanilla until blended. Set aside.
3. In a separate bowl combine the self-raising flour and oats. Add coconut.
4. Combine wet and dry ingredients until moist.
5. Drop a large teaspoon of biscuit mix on a greased or lined baking tray, about 2-4cm apart.
6. Bake for 10 minutes or until golden. Remove from oven immediately – if overcooked, biscuits become hard.

## Hummus

2 cups pre-cooked chickpeas
¼ cup oil
2 cloves garlic, peeled, or to taste
salt and freshly ground black pepper to taste
juice of 1 lemon, plus more as needed

1. Place all ingredients into a blender or food processor and blend until smooth.

**VARIATION - IF AVAILABLE FUNDS**

Add chopped fresh parsley leaves for garnish.

Add 1 tablespoon ground cumin or paprika, or to taste, plus a sprinkling for garnish.

Use olive or another flavoured oil.

## Easy Mayonnaise

1 large egg at room temperature
1 tbs white vinegar
¼ tsp salt
1 cup (240 ml) oil
1 tsp fresh lemon juice (optional)
1 tbs Dijon mustard (optional)

1. Add egg, vinegar, and salt to the small bowl and beat very well.
2. Add the oil in tiny drops until about a quarter of the oil has been added.
3. Once you notice that the mixture is beginning to thicken, slowly add the rest of the oil.

# MENU: Fortnight 2

| Week 3 | SUN | MON | TUES | WED | THURS | FRI | SAT |
|---|---|---|---|---|---|---|---|
| Breakfast | Pancakes and syrup or cinnamon and sugar | Wheat Breakfast Biscuits and/or Toast | Porridge | Pancakes and syrup or cinnamon and sugar | Porridge | Wheat Breakfast Biscuits and/or Toast | Boiled/scrambled egg (6) and Toast |
| Morning tea | Rice cakes and banana | Apple/fruit in season and Apple and Jam Rolls | Pikelets and jam | Wheat Breakfast Biscuits with butter and jam | Apple/fruit in season and Jelly tub | Anzac Biscuits and ½ carrot, cut in sticks | Yoghurt and jelly |
| Lunch | Toasted cheese sandwich | Fried rice with peas, carrot and ham | Sandwich with jam or ham 3 x cheese cubes | Sandwich with jam ½ carrot cut in sticks | Fried rice | Sandwich with jam or ham Apple/fruit in season | Couscous and veg (carrot and tomato) |
| Afternoon tea | Porridge with jam, yoghurt and cinnamon | Ham and cheese open grill | Rice cakes and tomato | Yoghurt and pineapple and coconut | Noodles or rice cakes | Open grilled cheese and sweet chilli sauce | Seasoned Spaghetti Pasta |
| Dinner | Country Chicken and Veg Pie | Chilli Con Carne with pasta | Satay or Butter Chicken and rice | 4-Egg Ham and Corn Quiche | Burgers | Stuffed Oven-Baked Potatoes | Shepherd's Pie |
| Dessert | Creamed Rice | | | | Custard and banana | | Pikelets and jam |

| Week 4 | SUN | MON | TUES | WED | THURS | FRI | SAT |
|---|---|---|---|---|---|---|---|
| Breakfast | Pancakes and syrup or cinnamon and sugar | Wheat Breakfast Biscuits and/or Toast | Porridge | Pancakes and syrup or cinnamon and sugar | Porridge | Wheat Breakfast Biscuits and/or Toast | Boiled/scrambled egg (6) and Toast |
| Morning tea | Open grilled cheese on toast | Jelly tub Rice cakes and cheese | ½ carrot cut into sticks and Apple and Jam Rolls | Wheat Breakfast Biscuits with butter and jam | Pikelets and jam | Anzac Biscuits Apple/fruit in season | Porridge with jam, yoghurt and cinnamon |
| Lunch | Fried Rice | Sandwich with jam Apple/fruit in season | Sandwich with jam or ham/tomato Anzac Biscuits | Sandwich with jam ½ carrot cut into sticks | Fried Rice | Sandwich with jam or tomato 3 x cubes cheese | Couscous and veg (carrot and tomato) |
| Afternoon tea | Noodles | Porridge with coconut and yoghurt | Rice cakes and tomato | Yoghurt and pineapple | Cheese and tomato open grill | Seasoned Spaghetti Pasta | Rice cakes and cheese |
| Dinner | Pita Pizzas | Tuna Mornay and Rice | Savoury Mince and Couscous | Stir Fry Chicken and Noodles | Pasta with Ham and Cheese Sauce | Spaghetti and Meatballs | Chilli Con Carne Nachos |
| Dessert | Creamed Rice | | Custard and banana | | Apple and Jam Rolls | | Creamed Rice |

# SHOPPING LIST: Fortnight 2

| QTY | Product | Check |
|---|---|---|
| 1 | Rolled Oats 900 g | |
| 1 | Breakfast Wheat Biscuits 1.2 kg | |
| 1 | Satay or Butter Chicken Simmer sauce 485 g | |
| 1 | Plain White Flour 1 kg | |
| 1 | Desiccated Coconut 500 g | |
| 3 | Canned Diced Tomatoes 400 g | |
| 1 | Whole Green Lentils 375 g | |
| 1 | Red Kidney Beans 400 g | |
| 1 | Tuna Chunks in Brine 185 g | |
| 2 | 2-minute Noodles 5 pack | |
| 1 | Long Grain Rice 1 kg | |
| 1 | Couscous 500 g | |
| 2 | Corn Kernels 420 g | |
| 2 | Corn Chips 200 g | |
| 2 | Rice Cakes 150 g | |
| 1 | Golden Syrup Squeeze 400 ml | |
| 1 | Italian Passata Sauce 690 g | |
| 1 | Fruit Spread (jam) 500 g | |
| 1 | Canned Pineapple in Natural Juice 440 g | |
| 1 | Jelly Crystals 85 g | |
| 2 | Cheese Sauce Mix 29 g | |
| 1 | Can Roast Meat Gravy Mix 120 g | |
| 1 | Sweet Chilli Sauce 500 ml | |
| 1 | Large Pasta Spirals 500 g | |
| 2 | Spaghetti Noodles 500 g | |
| | **Fruit and Vegetables** | |
| 20 | Apples | |
| 1 | 1 kg Brown Onions | |
| 1 | 1.5 kg bag Prepacked Carrots | |
| 1 | Bag Coleslaw Salad 200 g | |
| 3 | Tomatoes | |
| 6 | Bananas | |
| 1 | 2 kg bag Washed Potatoes | |
| | **Cold and Frozen** | |
| 1 | 250g Thinly Sliced Deli Ham | |

| QTY | Product | Check |
|---|---|---|
| 1 | 3-star Beef Mince 1 kg | |
| 1 | Sausage Mince 500 g | |
| 1 | 400 g Chicken Breast Fillets | |
| 1 | 150 g Diced Deli Ham | |
| 1 | Cooked Roast Chicken | |
| 1 | Tasty Cheddar Cheese Block 1 kg | |
| 1 | Butter Spread 500 g | |
| 1 | Vanilla Yoghurt 1 kg | |
| 3 | 2 L Full Cream Milk | |
| 2 | Caged Egg 12 pack 700 g | |
| 2 | Frozen Mixed Vegetables 1 kg | |
| 1 | Frozen Peas 1 kg | |
| 1 | Frozen Puff Pastry 6 Pack 1 kg | |
| | **Bread** | |
| 1 | Lebanese Bread Large 5 pack | |
| 7 | White Sandwich Loaf 700 g | |

# TIPS FOR MANAGING THIS FORTNIGHT OF COOKING

**Reminder**: Budget cooking means bulk recipes, portion control and using less expensive items such as lentils to add the protein to a meal but at a much cheaper cost than meat. It also means you need to get ready with food preparation and read recipes ahead as you may need to save something for another meal.

Get ready for this fortnight:

- Consider putting the money aside to purchase your bread and/or milk every few days so they are fresh. While you are there, your children might be able to grab a free piece of fruit if your supermarket offers this for children.
- Soak the brown lentils overnight, as this will cut down on cooking time. Keep the bag for cooking instructions. When cooked, divide evenly into 3 bags for Chilli Con Carne, Savory Mince and Shepherd's Pie. Freeze if they won't be used in the next few days.
- Only use half a sachet of seasoning per noodle pack so the other half can be used in other recipes.
- It is usually much cheaper to buy ham at the deli than pre-packaged ham. This may be the same for chicken breast, so it can be good to check this.
- If taking tomato with you during the day, take it in a separate container and assemble at work or school.
- Divide the mince into:
  - » 1 x 300 g for the Chilli Con Carne
  - » 1 x 300 g for the Savoury Mince and Couscous
  - » 1 x 300 g for the Shepherd's Pie
  - » 1 x 100 g for the Pita Pizzas.
- Divide diced ham into:
  - » 1 x 65 g for the Pasta with Ham and Cheese Sauce
  - » 1 x 65 g for Ham and Corn Quiche
  - » 1x 20 g for Fried Rice.
- Divide chicken into:
  - » 1 x 400 g for the Butter Chicken
  - » 1 x 100 g for the Pita Pizzas.
- Divide cheese into:
  - » 1 x 200 g block for Pita Pizza
  - » 4 x 100 g blocks for Spaghetti, Stuffed Potatoes, Pasta with Ham and Cheese Sauce, and Quiche
  - » 1 x 250 g block for sandwiches and open grills
  - » 1 x 150 g cubes.
- When you make up jelly, pour into small tubs or containers so it can be eaten away from home if needed.
- Freeze any leftovers for cook-free meals.

**IF THERE IS ADDITIONAL MONEY IN THE BUDGET:**

- Swap white bread for wholemeal or wholegrain bread, or wholegrain sourdough.
- Purchase extra eggs, sliced ham or chicken to add to sandwiches.
- Always add more fruit and vegetables as you can afford them, with the aim of eating 2 serves of fruit and 5 or more serves of vegetables each day per person. Choose a variety of colours of fruit and vegetables.

*Meatballs* (Image © Gary Perkin)

# RECIPES: Fortnight 2

## Country Chicken and Veg Pie

2 sheets frozen pastry
½ cooked BBQ chicken
1 diced carrot
½ diced onion
½ cup peas
20 g butter
2 tbs flour
2 tbs milk
¼-½ cup water

1. Place 1 sheet of pastry in a buttered pie dish.
2. Pull the meat from the cooked chicken and place in a bowl with carrot, onion and peas.
3. Melt butter in a small saucepan over low heat. When melted, add flour and cook for about a minute, stirring constantly. Add milk and enough water so it thickens to a sauce consistency, all the while still stirring.
4. Add to chicken mixture in bowl. Place sauce and chicken mixture onto pastry in a pie dish.
5. Top with other pastry sheet and seal around edges. Bake in 180°C oven until pastry is golden.
6. Serve with 2 or 3 diced, boiled potatoes.

**VARIATION - IF AVAILABLE FUNDS**
Add corn, diced sweet potato or green beans if you have some available.

## Chilli Con Carne

¾ packet of spiral pasta
1 diced onion
300 g beef mince
⅓ pack (pre-cooked) green lentils
1 can kidney beans, drained and rinsed
1 can diced tomatoes
⅓ bottle of sweet chilli sauce

1. Boil water, add pasta, and boil until soft.
2. In a large saucepan fry onion in a little butter till golden.
3. Add mince and fry until cooked.
4. Add to all other ingredients and simmer until it becomes a little thicker.

NB *Freeze some Chilli Con Carne to use on Nachos later – about ½ cup.

5. Serve on a bed of pasta.

**VARIATION - IF AVAILABLE FUNDS**
If you prefer you can serve with rice, couscous or if extra cash with quinoa.

## Satay or Butter Chicken and Rice

½ BBQ chicken
½ diced onion
1 large carrot, diced
1 jar butter chicken or satay chicken sauce
1 cup rice

1. Place rice in a large saucepan of water and boil until soft.
2. Pull the meat from cooked chicken and place in another saucepan with onion, carrot and butter chicken or satay sauce. Simmer until heated through. Serve with rice.

*Chilli Con Carne* (Image © Robyn McKenzie)

## 4-Egg Ham and Corn Quiche

1 sheet frozen pastry
½ can corn
65 g diced ham
4 eggs
2 tbs of milk
2 tbs flour

1. Place pastry sheet in buttered flan/pie dish.
2. Spread corn and ham over pastry base.
3. Beat eggs, milk and flour and pour over base.
4. Place in 180°C oven and cook until golden – about 30-40 mins.
5. Serve with thinly sliced potatoes that can cook in the oven at the same time as quiche, and with mixed veg.

## Burgers and Meatballs

7 slices of bread, torn into small pieces or crumbed in a food processor
1 onion, finely chopped
1 potato, grated
1 carrot, grated
500 g sausage mince

1. Mix all ingredients together, shape into 12 small meatballs and 9 rissoles (with floured hands to stop sticking).

Frugal Food | 17

2. Place on a baking tray and bake in 200°C oven until cooked.
3. Be aware meatballs will cook faster than rissoles.
4. Freeze meatballs for Spaghetti and Meatballs in Week 2.

**SERVING OPTIONS**

Serve burgers with tomato and coleslaw sandwiched between two slices of bread, or with potato and vegetables. Use meatballs in Spaghetti and Meatballs recipe.

**VARIATION - IF AVAILABLE FUNDS**

If extra funds, purchase other burger fillings such as beetroot, bacon, lettuce or pineapple.

## Spaghetti and Meatballs

½ packet of spaghetti
12 meatballs
¾ jar of Italian passata sauce (retain ¼ jar for pizza)
100 g cheese, grated

1. In a saucepan, boil water. Add spaghetti and boil until cooked.
2. In another saucepan, simmer meatballs and ¾ jar of Italian passata sauce over low heat.
3. Place spaghetti in bowls and spoon over sauce and meatballs. Top with some grated cheese.

**VARIATION - IF AVAILABLE FUNDS**

Add chopped onion and/or garlic and a variety of herbs if available.

## Stuffed Oven-Baked Potatoes

4 medium to large potatoes
½ onion
2-4 tbsp sweet chilli sauce
1 bag of coleslaw mix
2 tsp butter
100 g grated cheese

1. Scrub potatoes and cut a cross in the top to about halfway through the potato. Wrap in foil and bake in the oven until soft.
2. Chop the onion very finely and mix with sweet chilli sauce and coleslaw.
3. When potatoes are cooked, remove from oven, open the foil and spoon ½ tsp of butter and ¼ of chilli coleslaw mixture into each. Top with a sprinkle of cheese and serve.

**VARIATION - IF AVAILABLE FUNDS**

Add grated beetroot, tomato, cooked mince, ham or tuna if you have extra cash.

## Shepherd's Pie

3 medium potatoes
20 g butter
1 tbs of milk
⅓ packet (pre-cooked) green lentils
1 onion
300 g beef mince
1 can diced tomatoes
1 cup gravy mix (made up according to tin)

1. Clean and dice potatoes and place in boiling water. Cook until soft.
2. Remove from heat, drain and mash with butter and milk. It can also be thinned out with a little water so it spreads well. Set aside.
3. In a large frypan, fry onion and mince until cooked, add cooked lentils and canned tomatoes.
4. Make up a cup of gravy according to the packet and add to frypan. Stir until thoroughly mixed.
5. Place meat mixture in a pie dish, top with mashed potato. Bake in 200°C oven for about 30 mins until potato is golden brown. Serve with carrots and/or mixed vegetables.

**VARIATION - IF AVAILABLE FUNDS**

Substitute potatoes with sweet potato for variety if you can afford and like them.

## Pita Pizzas

¼ jar Italian passata sauce
½ can drained diced tomatoes
pita bread
100 g cooked mince
100 g chicken breast, cooked and chopped
sweet chilli sauce
200 g cheese

*Pasta with Ham and Cheese Sauce* (Image © Annilein)

1. Mix passata sauce and tomatoes together and then spread over pita breads. Add mince, chicken, and sweet chilli sauce. Top with cheese and place under medium griller until cheese has melted, and edges are crisp.

## Tuna Mornay and Rice

1 cup of rice
20 g butter
½ onion, diced
2 tbs flour
½ tsp mustard (optional)
½ cup milk
¼-½ cup water
1 packet cheese sauce
½ cup corn
185 g can of tuna (drained)

1. Cook rice according to packet instructions; boil until soft.
2. Melt butter in a large saucepan. Fry diced onion until soft. Add flour (and mustard if using) and stir for 30 seconds. Add milk, stirring constantly for about 1-2 minutes, adding enough water to make a medium sauce.
3. Make up cheese sauce to a thicker than normal consistency (by adding slightly less water) and add corn and tuna. Combine with onion mixture. Continue stirring until well mixed. Serve on a bed of rice.

## Savoury Mince and Couscous

1 diced onion
1 tsp of butter
300 g beef mince
⅓ packet (pre-cooked) green lentils
1 cup of frozen mixed vegetables
1 tbs of sweet chilli sauce
1 packet of seasoning from one of the noodle packs
1 cup dry couscous

1. In a large saucepan fry onion in 1 tsp butter until golden.
2. Add mince and cook until done.
3. Add all other ingredients except couscous and cook, stirring until vegetables are cooked.
4. Make up couscous according to box instructions.
5. Place couscous on plate and top with savoury mince.

## Stir Fry Chicken and Noodles

300 g chicken breast
2 cups of mixed vegetables
2 packets of 2-minute noodles
Soy sauce to taste

1. Dice chicken into small pieces and fry in a little butter until golden.

*Shepherd's Pie, p18*  (Image © JosephGough)

2. Add vegetables and continue cooking, stirring frequently.
3. Make up noodles according to pack directions, using 1 packet of seasoning only, mixed through both packets of noodles. When noodles are soft stir through chicken and veg, adding soy sauce to taste as desired.

## Pasta with Ham and Cheese Sauce

½ packet of spiral pasta
1 packet of cheese sauce
¾ of a 420 g can of corn, drained
65 g diced ham
100 g grated cheese

*Savoury Mince* (Image © Stargatechris)

Frugal Food | 19

*4-Egg Ham and Corn Quiche, p17* (Image © Danelle McCollum)

1. In saucepan, boil water and add spiral pasta. Boil until cooked.
2. Boil kettle and make cheese sauce according to packet.
3. Drain pasta, then add the corn, ham, and cheese sauce.
4. Simmer on low heat until all ingredients are hot. Serve topped with cheese.

**VARIATION - IF AVAILABLE FUNDS**
Add celery, broccoli or beans for texture and flavour.

## Chilli Con Carne Nachos

2 bags of corn chips
Chilli Con Carne sauce (kept from Chilli meal)
½ can diced tomatoes
¼ of 420 g can of corn
1 carrot, grated
300 g grated cheese
sweet chilli sauce

1. Lay out corn chips on dinner plates.
2. Mix together the heated Chilli Con Carne sauce and diced tomatoes.
3. Share out over the top of corn chips. Sprinkle with corn, carrot, and cheese. Drizzle with sweet chilli sauce.
4. Place under the grill or in the microwave until cheese is melted.

**VARIATION - IF AVAILABLE FUNDS**
Add spinach leaves and dollops of sour cream if you have extra cash.

## Fried Rice

2 cups rice
1 tsp butter
½ finely chopped onion
¼ cup peas
¼ cup carrots, finely chopped
small handful of diced ham
1 tbs oil
½ sachet of seasoning from a noodle packet

1. Boil rice until soft, and drain. (Leave to sit in the fridge for an hour or more if you have time.)
2. Heat butter in a frypan, add onion and cook until tender. Add peas, carrots and ham and cook over low heat, stirring until well mixed.
3. Add oil to the frypan with seasoning and rice. Continue stirring over low heat until well mixed and heated through.

**VARIATION - IF AVAILABLE FUNDS**
Add 1 large egg, if available. Move vegies over to one side of the pan, crack the egg into the opposite side and scramble until cooked and mix through the rice.

## Seasoned Spaghetti Pasta

60 g per person spaghetti pasta
½ packet of seasoning from a noodle packet

1. Place water in a saucepan and bring to boil; add spaghetti and simmer until just soft.
2. Drain and stir through seasoning.

## Apple and Jam Rolls

3 sheets of frozen pastry
your favourite jam
1-2 apples, sliced thinly or diced
desiccated coconut

1. Cut each sheet of pastry into 6 pieces – total of 18 pieces.
2. Arrange the pieces on a greased baking tray.
3. Spread each piece with jam, add some apple, and sprinkle with coconut.
4. Roll diagonally from the corner.

5. Bake in a moderate oven until golden brown.

NB: These can also be made without the apple if you wish.

## Anzac Biscuits

1 cup rolled oats
¾ cup desiccated coconut
1 cup plain flour, sifted
1 cup sugar
125 g butter, melted
2 tbs golden syrup
½ tsp bicarbonate of soda
3 tbs boiling water

1. Place the oats, coconut, flour and sugar in a bowl. Stir to combine.
2. Melt the butter and golden syrup in a saucepan over low heat.
3. In a separate bowl, combine the bicarb soda and boiling water, then add this to the butter/syrup mixture.
4. Pour this (foaming) mixture into your dry mix and stir.
5. When well combined, roll into golf ball-sized balls, drop onto a tray, spacing them about 6cm apart, and flatten a little with hand.
6. Bake for 15-18 minutes or until golden brown.

## Custard

⅛ cup custard powder
1 ¼ cups milk
1 tbs caster sugar

1. Combine custard powder and ¼ cup of the milk in a small jug. Stir until smooth.
2. Place custard mixture, sugar and remaining milk in a small saucepan over medium-low heat, stirring constantly until custard comes to the boil and thickens. Simmer, stirring for 1 minute.

## Creamed Rice

2 cups milk
½ tsp vanilla essence
1-2 cups water
⅓ cup sugar
¾ cup uncooked white medium-grain rice

1. Boil rice as per packet until just soft.
2. Combine milk, vanilla and sugar in a medium saucepan, stirring over medium heat until sugar dissolves.
3. Turn down to a low simmer and add cooked rice. Cook partially covered over low heat, stirring occasionally, for 40 minutes or until rice is tender and creamy, adding more water as needed. Serve warm or cold, and with fruit if desired.

**VARIATION - IF AVAILABLE FUNDS**

Add coconut and/or chocolate powder along with milk in a saucepan.

## Pancakes or Pikelets

2 cups flour
1 tsp sugar
2 eggs, lightly beaten
1 cup milk
½-1 cup water
50 g butter, melted

1. In a bowl, whisk flour and sugar.
2. Beat in the egg and then milk a little at a time until batter is smooth and lump-free.
3. Melt a little butter in a hot pan over medium heat and pour in batter to cover the base.
4. When bubbles form on the surface, flip the pancake over and cook until lightly golden on the other side.

For pikelets, just make smaller pancakes about the size of a tumbler glass bottom.

*Anzac Biscuits* (Image © Kate Crowley Smith)

# MENU: Fortnight 3

| Week 5 | SUN | MON | TUES | WED | THURS | FRI | SAT |
|---|---|---|---|---|---|---|---|
| Breakfast | Pancakes and syrup or cinnamon and sugar | Wheat Breakfast biscuits | Porridge and/or Toast | Wheat Breakfast Biscuits Toast | Porridge and/or Toast | Wheat Breakfast Biscuits | Boiled/scrambled egg (6) and Toast |
| Morning tea | Creamed Rice and Anzac Biscuits | Jelly tub and Pikelets and jam | Anzac Biscuits Banana | Apple/fruit in season and Rice crackers | Rice cakes and cheese | Anzac Biscuits and Apple/fruit in season | Grilled cheese on toast |
| Lunch | Porridge with yoghurt and pineapple | Sandwich with jam or ham Apple/fruit in season | Fried rice | Sandwich with jam or ham, ½ carrot cut into sticks | Couscous and veg (carrot and corn) | Sandwich with jam 3x cheese cubes | Seasoned Spaghetti Pasta |
| Afternoon tea | Wheat Breakfast Biscuits with butter and jam | Yoghurt and pineapple | Ham and cheese open grill | Anzac Biscuits Yoghurt | Cheese and sweet chilli sauce open grill | Rice cakes and tomato | Noodles |
| Dinner | Lettuce and tuna wraps | Burritos | Meat Pie | Sweet Chilli, Corn and Ham Fritters | Vegetarian Lasagne | Tacos | BBQ: Sausages/fried onion |
| Dessert | Custard | | Apple and Jam Rolls | | Yoghurt and Pineapple | | Creamed Rice |

| Week 6 | SUN | MON | TUES | WED | THURS | FRI | SAT |
|---|---|---|---|---|---|---|---|
| Breakfast | Pancakes and syrup or cinnamon and sugar | Wheat Breakfast Biscuits | Porridge and/or Toast | Wheat Breakfast Biscuits | Porridge and/or Toast | Wheat Breakfast Biscuits | Boiled/scrambled egg (6) and Toast |
| Morning tea | Rice crackers | Apple/fruit in season and Pikelets and jam | Anzac Biscuits Banana | Rice cakes and cheese | Anzac biscuit and ½ carrot cut into sticks | Yoghurt and Coconut | Grilled cheese on toast |
| Lunch | Sandwich with jam 3 x cheese cubes | Sandwich with jam or cheese ½ carrot cut into sticks | Couscous with butter, tomato and ham | Sandwich with cheese and ½ carrot cut into sticks | Fried rice | Sandwich with jam or cheese Apple/fruit in season | Couscous and mixed veg |
| Afternoon tea | Anzac Biscuits | Noodles or sandwich | Porridge with jam, coconut and yoghurt | Grilled cheese on toast | Rice cakes or noodles | Seasoned Spaghetti Pasta | Anzac Biscuits |
| Dinner | Special Fried Rice (with Egg) | Sausage and Veg Parcels | Spring Pasta with Ham | Fish Cakes | Traditional Lasagne | Satay Sausages and Rice | Smoked Salmon Quiche |
| Dessert | Yoghurt and jelly | | Apple and Jam Rolls | | Jelly and custard | | Creamed Rice |

# SHOPPING LIST: Fortnight 3

| QTY | Product | Check |
|---|---|---|
| 1 | Breakfast Wheat Biscuits 1.2 kg | |
| 1 | Rolled Oats 900 g | |
| 1 | Plain White Flour 1 kg | |
| 1 | Mexican Seasoning/ Taco Mix | |
| 3 | Canned Chopped Tomatoes 400 g | |
| 1 | Whole Green Lentils 375 g | |
| 2 | Italian Passata Sauce 690 g | |
| 1 | Pink Salmon in Spring Water 95 g | |
| 1 | Long Grain Rice 1 kg | |
| 1 | Tuna in Springwater 425 g | |
| 1 | Tuna in Brine 185 g | |
| 1 | Corn Kernels 420 g | |
| 1 | Lasagne Sheets 375 g | |
| 1 | Satay Simmer Sauce 485 g | |
| 2 | Rice Cakes 150 g | |
| 1 | Golden Syrup Squeeze 400 ml | |
| 1 | Fruit Spread (Jam) 500 g | |
| 1 | Canned Pineapple 440 g | |
| 1 | Jelly Crystals 85 g | |
| 1 | Cheese Sauce Mix 29 g | |
| 2 | 2-Minute Noodles 5 Pack | |
| 1 | Taco Shells 12 Pack | |
| 1 | Spaghetti Pasta | |
| 1 | Large Pasta Spirals 500 g | |
| 1 | Wraps (Wholemeal or White) 8 Pack | |
| | **Fruit And Vegetables** | |
| 20 | Apples | |
| 1 | 1 kg Brown Onions | |
| 8 | Bananas | |
| 1 | 2 kg Bag Washed Potatoes | |
| 1 | 500 g Pumpkin | |
| 1 | Lettuce | |
| 1 | Carrots Pre-Packed 1 kg | |
| 1 | ½ kg Tomatoes | |
| 1 | 1 Piece Broccoli Or ½ Cauliflower | |
| | **Cold And Frozen** | |
| 4 | 2 L Full Cream Milk | |

| QTY | Product | Check |
|---|---|---|
| 1 | 1.25 kg Chicken Breast Drumsticks | |
| 1 | Tray of BBQ Sausages 1.8 kg | |
| 1 | 3 Star Beef Mince 1 kg | |
| 1 | 250g Thinly Sliced Deli Ham | |
| 1 | Butter Blend Tub Salt Reduced 500g | |
| 1 | Tasty Cheddar Cheese Block 1 kg | |
| 2 | Caged Egg 12 Pack 700 g | |
| 1 | Vanilla Yoghurt 1 kg | |
| 1 | Frozen Beans 1 kg | |
| 1 | Frozen Peas 1 kg | |
| 2 | Frozen Puff Pastry 6 Pack 1 kg | |
| | **Bread** | |
| 6 | White Sandwich Loaf 700 g | |

## TIPS FOR MANAGING THIS FORTNIGHT OF COOKING

**Reminder**: Budget cooking means bulk recipes, portion control and using less expensive items such as lentils to add the protein to a meal but at a much cheaper cost than meat. It also means you need to get ready with food preparation and read recipes ahead as you may need to save something for another meal.

Get ready for the fortnight:

- Consider putting the money aside to purchase your bread and/or milk every few days so they are fresh. While you are there, your children might be able to grab a free piece of fruit if your supermarket offers this for children.

- Soak the brown lentils overnight, as this will cut down on cooking time. Keep the bag for cooking instructions. When cooked, divide evenly into 3 bags for Burritos/Tacos, Meat Pie and Lasagne. Freeze if they won't be used in the next few days.

- Divide the mince into:
    » 1 x 500g for the Burritos and Tacos
    » 1 x 250g for the Tasty Homemade Meat Pie
    » 1 x 250g for the Traditional Lasagne.

- Divide ham into:
    » 1 x 50g for the Chilli Corn and Ham Fritters
    » 1 x 200g for sandwiches.

- Divide cheese into:
    » 2 x 250g blocks for Tacos and Burritos
    » 3 x 100g blocks for Traditional Lasagne, Vegetarian Lasagne and Spring Pasta
    » 1 x 250g block for sandwiches and open grills
    » 1 x 150g block for cheese cubes.

- When you make up jelly, pour into small tubs or containers so it can be eaten away from home if needed.

- Freeze any leftovers for cook-free meals.

**IF THERE IS ADDITIONAL MONEY IN THE BUDGET:**

- Swap white bread for wholemeal or wholegrain bread, or wholegrain sourdough.

- Purchase extra eggs, sliced ham or chicken to add to sandwiches.

- Always add more fruit and vegetables as you can afford them, with the aim of eating 2 serves of fruit and 5 or more serves of vegetables each day per person. Choose a variety of colours of fruit and vegetables.

*Fish Cakes, p27* (Image © Svetlana Verbitckaia)

*Vegetarian Lasagne* (Image © stckcreations)

## RECIPES: Fortnight 3

### Lettuce Tuna Wraps

18-20 lettuce leaves
1 cup of rice
1 packet seasoning
1 x 185 g can of tuna in brine
1 carrot, grated
2 tbs sweet chilli sauce

1. Wash lettuce and set aside.
2. Cook rice until soft, adding 1 packet of seasoning from a noodle packet.
3. Mix tuna, rice and carrot with sweet chilli sauce.
4. Spoon evenly into lettuce leaves and roll into thick cigar-like rolls with the end tucked in.
5. Serve with extra sweet chilli sauce for dipping if desired.

### Tacos and Burritos

⅓ pack of green lentils
1 diced onion
500 g of beef mince
1 packet taco seasoning mix
1 cup water
250 g grated cheese (each meal)
1 chopped tomato (each meal)
shredded lettuce

1. Boil lentils until soft. (If you soak overnight, cooking time is less.)
2. In a large frypan, fry onion in a little butter.
3. When onion is golden add mince and cook until done.
4. Add 1 packet of taco seasoning mixed with 1 cup water.
5. Simmer until gravy thickens.
6. Divide mince mixture: half for Burritos and other half for Tacos.
7. If having tacos use taco shells and if having burritos use burrito wraps.
8. Serve with grated cheese, shredded lettuce and chopped tomatoes.

### Tasty Homemade Meat Pie

2 sheets frozen pastry
⅓ packet of lentils
1 diced onion
250 g beef mince
1 diced potato
1 diced carrot
1 can diced tomatoes
1 cup gravy, made up to a thick consistency

1. Place 1 sheet of pastry in a buttered pie dish.
2. Boil lentils until soft and then drain. Set aside.
3. In frying pan, fry onion and mince until cooked. Place in a bowl with carrot, potato, lentils and diced tomatoes. Mix well. Stir in thick gravy.
4. Pour into pastry and top with another pastry sheet. Pierce with a fork a few times and seal around the edges with fork or thumb.
5. Bake in 200°C oven until pastry is golden. Serve with peas and potato fries baked in the oven while the pie cooked.

### Vegetarian Lasagne

1 chopped onion
1 medium chopped potato
100 g chopped pumpkin
1 finely chopped carrot
½ head broccoli, chopped
½ can diced tomatoes

Frugal Food | 25

1 jar of passata sauce
20 g butter
2 tbs flour
250 ml milk
6 sheets of instant lasagne
½ packet of cheese sauce
100g grated cheese

1. In a large saucepan, fry chopped onion in a little butter. When transparent, add potato, pumpkin, carrot and broccoli. Cook with a little water until a little soft.
2. Add diced tomatoes and passata sauce to vegie mixture and continue cooking on low, stirring regularly for a further 5 mins.
3. In a saucepan, melt butter. Remove from heat, add flour and stir until mixed well. Return to low heat and slowly stir in milk. While simmering, stir continuously until white sauce thickens slightly. If it thickens too much add some water and continue simmering and stirring until is a medium consistency. Set aside.
4. In an ovenproof lasagne dish, spread a third of the tomato mixture over the bottom, cover with lasagne sheets, then with white sauce. Continue layering tomato mixture, pasta sheets and white sauce 2 more times. Top with made up half-packet of cheese sauce and with cheese.
5. Bake in 180°C oven until golden brown. Serve with salad or vegetables.

## BBQ Sausages

9-10 sausages
1-2 onions sliced

1. Enjoy a BBQ with sausages and fried onion.
2. Serve with bread and/or salad.

## Special Fried Rice (with Egg)

2 cups rice
½ finely chopped onion
¼ cup peas
¼ cup carrots, finely chopped
small handful of diced ham
2 tbs oil
½ sachet of seasoning from a noodle packet

1. Boil rice until soft, and drain. (Leave to sit in the fridge for an hour or more if you have time)
2. Heat 1 tbs oil in a frypan, add onion and cook until tender. Add peas, carrots and ham and cook over low heat, stirring until well mixed.
3. Add 1 tbs oil to the frypan with seasoning and rice. Continue stirring over low heat until well mixed and heated through.
4. Add 1 large egg, if available. Move vegies over to one side of the pan, crack the egg into the opposite side and scramble until cooked and mix through the rice.
5. Add sweet chilli sauce and/or soy sauce to taste.

## Sausage and Veg Parcels

3 sausages, cooked and sliced fairly fine
2 cups of mixed veg
1 cup of made up gravy, fairly thick
3 sheets of pastry, cut into quarters

1. Mix sliced sausages, veg and gravy in a bowl.
2. Place spoonfuls of mixture onto each ¼ sheet of pastry.
3. Pull pastry corners together and seal in the centre by squeezing.
4. Place on a greased baking tray, paint a little milk on each and place in 180°C oven. Bake until golden.
5. Serve with beans and mashed pumpkin.

## Spring Pasta with Ham

300 g of pasta spirals
1 cup peas
1 grated carrot
1 chopped tomato

*Lettuce Tuna Wraps, p25* (Image © Fotografieberlin)

26 | Frugal Food

100 g diced ham

1 packet of instant cheese sauce mix, made up according to instructions

100 g grated cheese

1. Bring a saucepan of water to the boil, add pasta spirals, and cook until still a little firm.
2. Add peas and cook for a further 3 minutes. Drain.
3. Add carrot and chopped tomato, ham, and made up cheese sauce. Simmer, stirring lightly for 1 minute. Serve immediately with grated cheese sprinkled over the top.

## Ovenbaked Chilli, Corn and Ham Fritters

1 ½ cups self-raising flour
¾ cup milk
1 egg
2 tbs of sweet chilli sauce
1 420 g can corn kernels
50 g ham, chopped

1. Preheat oven to 200°C.
2. Double-sift the flour into a bowl.
3. Using a fork, whisk milk and egg together in a jug until combined. Pour over the flour. Stir until smooth.
4. Add sweet chilli sauce, corn and ham and stir until well combined.
5. Grease a baking tray well with butter.
6. Drop mixture (the size of approx. 2 dessert spoons to make 1 fritter) onto a tray.
7. Bake until firm. Transfer to a wire rack to cool. Serve with salad.

**TIPS**

You can also shallow fry these in a frying pan if you have some oil available.

*Sausage and Veg Parcels, p26* (Image © Viktofischer)

Replace corn with grated zucchini for variety if you like, or to add extra nutrition.

## Fish Cakes

6 medium potatoes, chopped
210 g canned tuna, drained
2 tbs of sweet chilli sauce
1 tsp butter
½ onion, finely chopped
2 tbs milk
½ cup flour

1. Boil chopped potatoes until soft. Mash until smooth.
2. Mix the tuna into the mashed potatoes with the sweet chilli sauce.
3. Melt butter in a pan, add onion and cook until transparent. (Add parsley and seasoning if you have them.)
4. Add the cooked onion to tuna mixture. Mix well and shape into 8 patties.
5. Dip the patties into the milk and then into the flour.
6. Bake on a greased baking tray until the outside is firm. Serve with veg or salad, accompanied by lemon and/or mayonnaise if you have any.

**VARIATION**

Alternatively, shallow fry in hot oil for a few minutes until golden brown.

## Traditional Lasagne

6 sheets of instant lasagne
1 chopped onion
250 g beef mince
⅓ packet of lentils
1 can diced tomatoes
1 jar of passata sauce
20 g butter
1 cup milk
2 tbs flour
100 g grated cheese

1. Fry chopped onion in a little butter until golden. Add mince and cook until cooked through.

Frugal Food | 27

*Smoked Salmon Quiche, p28 (Image © Coconutsdreams)*

2. In a bowl, mix lentils, diced tomatoes and passata sauce. Add to cooked mince and onion and continue cooking on simmer, stirring regularly.
3. In a saucepan, melt butter, remove from heat, add flour and stir until mixed well. Return to low heat and stir in milk. Stir continuously while simmering until white sauce thickens slightly. If it thickens too much add some water and continue simmering until it is a medium consistency sauce. Set aside.
4. In an ovenproof lasagne dish, spread a third of the meat sauce over the bottom, cover with lasagne sheets, then white sauce. Continue layers of meat, pasta sheets and white sauce 2 more times. Top with cheese.
5. Bake in 180°C oven until golden brown. Serve with salad.

## Satay Sausages and Rice

1 cup rice
4-5 sausages
1 chopped potato
1 finely diced carrot
1 jar of satay simmer sauce

1. Place rice in a large saucepan of water and boil until soft.
2. Grill sausages until cooked, then slice.
3. Place chopped potato and carrot in a saucepan of boiling water. Cook until just soft; drain.
4. Place all vegetables into a saucepan with sliced cooked sausages. Add satay sauce and simmer until heated through. Serve with rice.

## Smoked Salmon Quiche

1 sheet frozen pastry
½ chopped onion
1 x 95 g can smoked salmon
4 eggs
4 tbs of milk

1. Place pastry sheet in buttered flan/pie dish. Fry chopped onion in a little butter until golden brown.
2. Spread onion and salmon over the pastry base. Beat egg and milk and pour over base.
3. Place in 180°C oven and cook until golden, about 30-40 mins.
4. Serve with thinly sliced potatoes that can be cooked in the oven at the same time as the quiche, and with mixed veg or salad.

**VARIATION - IF AVAILABLE FUNDS**

Add spinach or broccoli.

## Seasoned Spaghetti Pasta

60 g per person spaghetti pasta
½ packet of seasoning from a noodle packet

1. Place water in a saucepan and bring to boil; add spaghetti and simmer until just soft.
2. Drain and stir through seasoning.

## Custard

⅛ cup custard powder
1 ¼ cups milk
1 tbs caster sugar

1. Combine custard powder and ¼ cup of the milk in a small jug. Stir until smooth.
2. Place custard mixture, sugar and remaining milk in a small saucepan over medium-low heat, stirring constantly until custard comes to the boil and thickens. Simmer, stirring for 1 minute.

## Apple and Jam Rolls

3 sheets of frozen pastry
your favourite jam
1-2 apples, sliced thinly or diced
desiccated coconut

1. Cut each sheet of pastry into 6 pieces – total of 18 pieces.
2. Arrange the pieces on a greased baking tray.
3. Spread each piece with jam, add some apple, and sprinkle with coconut.
4. Roll diagonally from the corner.

5. Bake in a moderate oven until golden brown.

NB: These can also be made without the apple if you wish.

## Anzac Biscuits

1 cup rolled oats
¾ cup desiccated coconut
1 cup plain flour, sifted
1 cup sugar
125 g butter, melted
2 tbs golden syrup
½ tsp bicarbonate of soda
3 tbs boiling water

1. Place the oats, coconut, flour and sugar in a bowl. Stir to combine.
2. Melt the butter and golden syrup in a saucepan over low heat.
3. In a separate bowl, combine the bicarb soda and boiling water, then add this to the butter/syrup mixture.
4. Pour this (foaming) mixture into your dry mix and stir.
5. When well combined, roll into golf ball-sized balls, drop onto tray spacing them about 6cm apart, and flatten a little with hand.
6. Bake for 15-18 minutes or until golden brown.

## Pancakes/ Pikelets

2 cups flour
1 tsp sugar
2 eggs, lightly beaten
1 cup milk
½-1 cup water
50 g butter, melted

1. In a bowl, whisk flour and sugar.
2. Beat in the egg and then milk a little at a time until batter is smooth and lump-free.
3. Melt a little butter in a hot pan over medium heat and pour in batter to cover the base.
4. When bubbles form on the surface, flip the pancake over and cook until lightly golden on the other side.

NB: For pikelets, just make smaller pancakes about the size of a tumbler glass bottom.

This recipe should make enough pancakes for breakfast and about a dozen small pikelets for dessert another day.

## Creamed Rice

¾ cup uncooked white medium-grain rice
2 cups milk
½ tsp vanilla essence
1-2 cups water
⅓ cup sugar

1. Boil rice as per packet until just soft.
2. Combine milk, vanilla and sugar in a medium saucepan, stirring over medium heat until sugar dissolves.
3. Turn down to a low simmer and add cooked rice. Cook, partially covered, over low heat, stirring occasionally, for 40 minutes or until rice is tender and creamy, adding more water as needed. Serve warm or cold, and with fruit if desired.

**VARIATION - IF AVAILABLE FUNDS**

Add coconut and/or chocolate powder along with milk in a saucepan.

*Pancakes* (Image © KrillKobyzev)

# MENU: Fortnight 4 – Vegetarian

| Week 7 | SUN | MON | TUES | WED | THURS | FRI | SAT |
|---|---|---|---|---|---|---|---|
| Breakfast | Pancakes with butter and sugar or syrup | Wheat Breakfast Biscuits | Porridge and/or Toast | Wheat Breakfast Biscuits | Porridge and/or Toast | Wheat Breakfast Biscuits | Bircher Muesli |
| Morning tea | Anzac Biscuits and apple | Rice cakes and tomato | Anzac Biscuits and banana | Pikelets and jam or syrup | Apple and Jam rolls | Anzac Biscuits and apple | Rice cakes and tomato |
| Lunch | Couscous with carrot and corn | Sandwich with peanut butter and cheese cubes | Fried rice | Sandwich and jam and carrot sticks | Spiral Pasta with Curry and Corn | Sandwich with peanut butter and cheese cubes | Toasted cheese sandwich |
| Afternoon tea | Anzac Biscuits and apple | Noodles or sandwich | Sandwich with jam or peanut butter | Grilled cheese on toast | Breakfast biscuits with butter and jam | Yoghurt and nut sprinkle | Seasoned Spaghetti Pasta |
| Dinner | Vegetarian Chilli | Stuffed Oven Baked Potato | Spinach and Corn Quiche | Creamy Coconut Vegetable Korma and rice | Nachos | Vegetarian Lasagne | Vegetarian Shepherd's Pie |
| Dessert | Creamed Rice | | Pikelets and jam or syrup | | | | Creamed Rice |

| Week 8 | SUN | MON | TUES | WED | THURS | FRI | SAT |
|---|---|---|---|---|---|---|---|
| Breakfast | Pancakes with butter and sugar or syrup | Wheat Breakfast Biscuits | Porridge and/or Toast | Wheat Breakfast Biscuits | Porridge and/or Toast | Wheat Breakfast Biscuits | Pancakes with butter and sugar or syrup |
| Morning tea | Grilled cheese on toast | Apple and Jam Rolls | Anzac Biscuits Banana | Rice cakes and cheese cubes | Apple and Jam Rolls | Anzac Biscuits Apple | Rice cakes and peanut butter |
| Lunch | Fried Rice | Sandwich with jam or peanut butter | Cheese and tomato on ½ pita wrap | Sandwich and jam and Carrot sticks | Fried Rice | Sandwich with jam and cheese cubes | Couscous with carrot and corn |
| Afternoon tea | Breakfast biscuits with butter and jam | Seasoned Spaghetti Pasta | Pikelets and jam | Apple and Anzac Biscuits | Breakfast biscuits and jam | Rice cakes and tomato | Noodles or sandwich |
| Dinner | Pita Pizzas | Oven Baked Chilli Corn Fritters | Rice Rissoles | Vegetarian Spaghetti | Cheesy Veg Pie | Easy Vegetarian Pie | Vegetarian Enchiladas |
| Dessert | Creamed Rice | | Yoghurt and nut sprinkle | | | Creamed Rice | |

# SHOPPING LIST: Fortnight 4 – Vegetarian

| QTY | Product | Check |
|---|---|---|
| 1 | Rolled Oats 1 kg | |
| 1 | Breakfast Wheat Biscuits 1.2 kg | |
| 1 | Curry Powder 50 g | |
| 1 | Turmeric 25 g | |
| 1 | Cumin 25 g | |
| 1 | Plain White Flour 1 kg | |
| 1 | Desiccated Coconut 500 g | |
| 1 | White Sugar 1 kg | |
| 1 | Crushed Peanuts 150 g | |
| 3 | Canned Diced Tomatoes 400 g | |
| 1 | Whole Green Lentils 375 g | |
| 3 | Red Kidney Beans 400 g | |
| 2 | 2-Minute Noodles 5 Pack | |
| 1 | Brown Rice 1 kg | |
| 1 | Long Grain Rice 1 kg | |
| 1 | Couscous 500 g | |
| 1 | Cheese Sauce Mix 29 g | |
| 3 | Corn Kernels 420 g | |
| 2 | Corn Chips 200 g | |
| 2 | Rice Cakes 150 g | |
| 1 | Golden Syrup Squeeze 400 ml | |
| 2 | Italian Passata Sauce 690 g | |
| 1 | Mexican Sauce 240 g | |
| 1 | Can Tomato Paste 170 g | |
| 1 | Can Coconut Milk 400 ml | |
| 1 | Fruit Spread (Jam) 500 g | |
| 1 | Peanut Butter 375 g | |
| 1 | Sweet Chilli Sauce 500 ml | |
| 1 | Wholemeal Wraps 416 g | |
| 2 | Spaghetti Noodles 500 g | |
| 1 | Instant Lasagne Sheets 250 g | |
| 1 | Large Pasta Spirals 500 g | |
| | **Fruit And Vegetables** | |
| 8 | Bananas | |
| 20 | Apples | |
| 1 | 1 kg Pre-Packed Brown Onions | |
| 1 | Coleslaw Salad Bag 200 g | |
| 1 | 3 kg Potatoes | |
| 3 | Medium Tomatoes | |
| 2 | Broccoli | |

| QTY | Product | Check |
|---|---|---|
| 1 | Piece Pumpkin 750 g | |
| 1 | Garlic Cloves | |
| 1 | 200 g Mushrooms | |
| 1 | Baby Spinach 60 g | |
| 1 | Carrots Pre-Packed 1.5 kg | |
| | **Cold and Frozen** | |
| 1 | Caged Eggs 12 Pack 700 g | |
| 1 | Tasty Cheddar Cheese Block 1 kg | |
| 2 | Butter Blend Tub Salt Reduced 500 g | |
| 1 | Vanilla Yoghurt 1 kg | |
| 3 | 2 L Full Cream Milk or 6 x Longlife 1 L Milk | |
| 1 | Frozen Peas 1 kg | |
| 2 | Frozen Mixed Vegetables 1 kg | |
| 1 | Frozen Puff Pastry 6 Pack 1 kg | |
| | **Bread** | |
| 1 | Lebanese Bread Large 5 Pack | |
| 7 | White Sandwich Loaf 700 g | |

## TIPS FOR MANAGING THIS FORTNIGHT OF COOKING

**Reminder**: Budget cooking means bulk recipes, portion control and using less expensive items such as lentils to add the protein to a meal at a much cheaper cost. It also means you need to get ready with food preparation and read recipes ahead as you may need to save something for another meal.

Get ready for the fortnight:

- Consider putting the money aside to purchase your bread and/or milk every few days so they are fresh. While you are there, your children might be able to grab a free piece of fruit if your supermarket offers this for children.

- Soak the brown lentils overnight, as this will cut down on cooking time. Keep the bag for cooking instructions. When cooked, divide evenly into 3 bags for Spaghetti, Chilli and Shepherd's Pie. Freeze if they won't be used in the next few days.

- Divide cheese into:
  » 2 x 200 g blocks for Nachos and Pizza
  » 2 x 100 g blocks for Vegetarian Lasagne and Vegetarian Enchiladas
  » 4 x 50 g blocks for Rice Rissoles, Stuffed Oven-Baked Potatoes, Cheesy Veg Pie and Vegetarian Spaghetti
  » 1 x 100 g block for sandwiches and open grills
  » 1 x 100 g block for cheese cubes.

- Freeze any leftovers for cook-free meals.

**IF THERE IS ADDITIONAL MONEY IN THE BUDGET:**

- Swap white bread for wholemeal or wholegrain bread, or wholegrain sourdough.

- Purchase extra eggs, tofu and nuts to add to meals.

- Always add more fruit and vegetables as you can afford them, with the aim of eating 2 serves of fruit and 5 or more serves of vegetables each day per person. Choose a variety of colours of fruit and vegetables.

(Image © Kate Crowley Smith)

# RECIPES: Fortnight 4 – Vegetarian

## Vegetarian Chilli

1 diced onion
⅓ pack pre-cooked green lentils
1 can kidney beans
1 grated carrot
1 can of diced tomatoes
30 g tomato paste
⅓ bottle of sweet chilli sauce
1 cup couscous

1. In a large saucepan, fry onion in a little butter.
2. When onion is golden, add pre-cooked lentils and beans, and cook until well combined.
3. Add all other ingredients except couscous and simmer, stirring for 5-10 mins or until it becomes a little thicker.
4. Prepare couscous according to packet directions.
5. Serve on a bed of couscous.

Keep some of the Vegetarian Chilli mixture to use on Nachos later – about ½ cup.

**VARIATION - IF AVAILABLE FUNDS**

Serve with rice, pasta or, if extra cash, with quinoa instead of couscous.

## Stuffed Oven-Baked Potatoes

4 medium to large potatoes
½ onion
2-4 tbs sweet chilli sauce
1 carrot, grated
150 g of coleslaw mix
2 tsp butter
50 g grated cheese

1. Scrub potatoes and cut a cross in the top about halfway through the potato. Wrap in foil and bake in the oven until soft.
2. Chop the onion very finely and mix with sweet chilli sauce, grated carrot and coleslaw.
3. When potatoes are cooked, remove from oven, open foil and spoon ½ teaspoon of butter and ¼ of chilli coleslaw mixture into each. Top with a sprinkle of cheese and serve.

**VARIATION - IF AVAILABLE FUNDS**

Add a range of vegetables.

Add a chilli mixture.

Add a good dollop of sour cream on each.

## Creamy Coconut Vegetable Korma

1½ cups brown rice
2 medium potatoes, diced
½ cup corn kernels
½ cup peas
2 carrots, diced
½ broccoli head, diced
2 cups mixed vegetables

**VEGETARIAN KORMA SAUCE**
1 tbs butter
1 large onion, chopped
4 garlic cloves, crushed
140 g of tomato paste

*Stuffed Oven-Baked Potatoes* (Image © Rlat)

1 tbs curry powder
1 ½ teaspoons each: cumin, turmeric
1 x 400 ml can of coconut milk
100 g crushed peanuts
1 tbs peanut butter
1¼ cups water
½ cup milk
1 tbs sugar
coconut for top

1. In a large saucepan, boil rice until cooked.
2. To a large pot add the potatoes, cover with water and bring to a boil. Let the potatoes boil for 5 minutes, then add the rest of the vegies to the pot. Let boil for another 5 minutes, then drain and set aside.
3. While the vegetables are cooking, melt the butter in another medium-sized pot. Add the onion and cook, stirring occasionally, until it is soft, about 5 minutes. Add the crushed garlic and cook for a further 2 minutes.
4. Remove the pot from the heat and add the tomato paste and all of the spices. Stir well, then

Frugal Food | 33

return the pot to the heat. When the spices are fragrant and the tomato paste has caramelised, after about 1 minute, add the coconut milk, nuts, peanut butter and 1 ¼ cups of water and let boil for a few minutes.

5. Stir in the milk and sugar and when well combined add this to the vegies. Serve immediately on bed of rice topped with a sprinkle of coconut.

## Nachos

2 bags of corn chips
Vegetarian Chilli sauce (kept from Vegetarian Chilli meal)
1 can diced tomatoes
sweet chilli sauce
1 carrot, grated
200 g of grated cheese

1. Lay out corn chips on heat-proof plates.
2. Mix together Vegetarian Chilli, diced tomatoes and sweet chilli sauce.
3. Share out over the top of corn chips along with grated carrot, sprinkle with cheese and place under the grill or in the microwave until cheese is melted.

## Vegetarian Lasagne

1 chopped onion
1 medium potato, chopped
100 g chopped pumpkin
1 finely chopped carrot
½ head broccoli, chopped
½ can diced tomatoes
50 g mushrooms, chopped
1 jar of passata sauce
20 g butter
2 tbs flour
250 ml milk
6 sheets of instant lasagne

½ packet of cheese sauce
100 g grated cheese

1. In a large saucepan, fry chopped onion in a little butter. When transparent add potato, pumpkin, carrot and broccoli. Cook with a little water until slightly softened.
2. Add diced tomatoes, chopped mushrooms, and passata sauce to the veg mixture and continue cooking on low, stirring regularly for a further 5 mins.
3. In a saucepan, melt butter, remove from heat, add flour and stir until mixed well. Return to low heat and slowly stir in milk. While simmering, stir continuously until white sauce thickens slightly. If it thickens too much, add some water and continue simmering and stirring until it is a medium consistency. Set aside.
4. In an ovenproof lasagne dish, spread one third of the tomato mixture over the bottom, cover with lasagne sheets, then cover with white sauce. Continue layering tomato mixture, pasta sheets and white sauce 2 more times.
5. Top with ½ packet of prepared cheese sauce and sprinkle with cheese. Bake in 180°C oven until golden brown. Serve with salad or vegetables.

## Vegetarian Shepherd's Pie

3 medium potatoes
20 g butter
1 tbs of milk
1 onion
⅓ packet pre-cooked green lentils
1 can diced tomatoes
1 diced carrot
1 cup gravy mix (made up according to directions)

1. Clean and dice potatoes and place in boiling water; cook until soft.
2. Remove from heat, drain, and mash with butter and milk.
3. In a large frypan, fry onion until cooked. Add pre-cooked lentils, canned tomatoes and diced carrot.
4. Make up a cup of gravy according to the packet directions, and add to frypan. Stir until thoroughly mixed.
5. Place mixture in a pie dish, and top with mashed potato. Bake in 200°C oven for about 30 mins until potato is golden brown. Serve with vegetables.

### VARIATION - IF AVAILABLE FUNDS

Use sweet potato instead of potato for the top if you have extra cash.

Add extra vegetables into the lentil mixture before covering with potato.

## Pita Pizzas

¼ jar passata sauce
½ can diced tomatoes
pita bread
¼ packet of spinach leaves
1 carrot, grated
sweet chilli sauce
200 g grated cheese

1. Mix passata sauce and tomatoes together. Spread over pita breads.
2. Add whatever toppings you like. Top with cheese and place under medium griller until cheese has melted and edges are crisp.

### VARIATION - IF AVAILABLE FUNDS

Add spinach leaves, feta cheese, fresh tomatoes, mushrooms or tofu if you have extra cash.

*Cheesy Veg Pie, p36  (Image © Ehrlif)*

## Oven-Baked Chilli Corn Fritters

**1 ½ cups self-raising flour**
**¾ cup milk**
**1 egg**
**2 tbs sweet chilli sauce**
**½ can corn kernels**
**1 small onion, finely chopped**
**¼ bag of spinach leaves**

1. Preheat oven to 200°C.
2. Double-sift the flour into a bowl. Using a fork, whisk milk and egg together in a jug until combined. Pour over the flour. Stir until smooth. Add sweet chilli sauce, corn, onion and spinach and stir until well combined.
3. Grease a baking tray well with butter, and spoon 2 dessert spoons of mixture per fritter onto the tray.
4. Bake until firm. Transfer to a wire rack to cool. Serve with mashed potato.

You can also shallow fry these in a frypan if you have some oil available.

**VARIATION - IF AVAILABLE FUNDS**

Add or replace corn with grated zucchini and/or carrot.

## Rice Rissoles

**50 g grated cheese**
**1 egg**
**1 tsp curry powder**
**4 tbs peanut butter**
**2 cloves garlic, crushed**
**chopped parsley to taste (optional)**
**grated black pepper**
**2 cups brown rice**
**flour to coat the rissoles**

1. Combine all ingredients except the rice and flour in a large bowl.
2. Steam or boil the rice till it is a bit "overcooked" and sticky.
3. Add the hot rice to the other ingredients and mix well – use your hands if necessary.
4. Shape into patties, roll in flour and brush them with a little oil/melted butter. Bake them in the oven, on a large oven tray, until golden.

**VARIATION - IF AVAILABLE FUNDS**

Prepare satay sauce with peanut butter, butter and ½ packet of seasoning from noodles.

## Vegetarian Spaghetti

**½ packet of spaghetti**
**1 chopped onion**
**⅓ packet of pre-cooked lentils**
**½ packet of noodle seasoning**
**¾ jar of passata sauce (retain ¼ jar for pizza)**
**1 can kidney beans, drained and washed**
**50 g grated cheese**

1. In a saucepan, boil water, add spaghetti, and boil until cooked.
2. In another saucepan add a little water and cook chopped onions until tender. Add pre-cooked lentils and seasoning and cook until well mixed.
3. Stir in ¾ jar of passata sauce and beans. Simmer over low heat until well combined.

*Creamy Coconut Vegetable Korma, p33* (Image © Paul Cowan)

4. Place spaghetti in bowls and spoon sauce over top. Finish with some grated cheese.

## Cheesy Veg Pie

1 medium potato
1 carrot, diced
100 g piece of pumpkin
½ cup peas
½ diced onion
½ can corn kernels
2 sheets frozen pastry
20 g butter
2 tbs flour
4 tbs milk
¼-½ cup water
½ packet cheese sauce
50 g grated cheese

1. Dice potato, carrot and pumpkin. Place in a saucepan, cover with water and boil until just softening.
2. In a large bowl combine cooked carrot, potato and pumpkin with peas, onion and corn.
3. Place 1 sheet of pastry into a buttered pie dish.
4. In another smaller saucepan, melt butter. When melted, remove from heat, add flour and stir well. Return to low heat and cook for about a minute, stirring constantly while slowly adding milk and enough water so it thickens to a sauce consistency.
5. Stir sauce through vegetable mixture in bowl. Place this mixture onto pastry in the pie dish.
6. Prepare ½ packet of cheese sauce and pour over veg mixture in pie dish. Sprinkle with cheese.
7. Cover with other pastry sheet and seal around edges. Bake in 180°C oven until pastry is golden.
8. Serve with thinly sliced potatoes that are baked in the oven while the pie is cooking.

## Easy Vegetarian Pie

4 tbs butter
4 slices bread
3 carrots, diced
50 g coleslaw mix
1 small onion, diced
150 g mushrooms, sliced
3 tbs flour
1 ½ cups milk
1 ½ cups water
1 cup frozen peas

1. Preheat the oven to 210°C. Melt the butter in a large frypan. When melted, remove 1 tbs into a small bowl – brush the bread with this melted butter and set aside.
2. Add the carrots, coleslaw mix and onion to the frypan. Cover and cook, stirring occasionally for about 5 minutes. Add the mushrooms; cover and continue cooking, stirring occasionally, for about 3 minutes. Add the flour and cook, stirring for 1 minute.
3. Add the milk and water, and stir until mixed well. Bring to a boil. Reduce the heat until mixture is simmering, and continue cooking for about 5 mins, stirring occasionally, until mixture thickens. Add the frozen peas and continue to simmer for a few more minutes. Remove from the heat and pour into an oven-proof dish. Cut the bread into quarters and arrange bread over the top, buttered side up.
4. Bake in the oven until the bread is toasted, about 8 minutes.

**VARIATION - IF AVAILABLE FUNDS**

If money permits you can add a 400 g package of extra-firm tofu, drained, patted dry and cut into ½-inch cubes. Add at the same time as the peas.

## Vegetarian Enchiladas

1 jar Mexican/enchilada sauce
1 can kidney beans, drained and rinsed
½ can corn kernels
1 chopped onion
1 cup chopped cooked broccoli
1 cup grated cheddar cheese

4-6 whole wheat tortillas

1. Grease a large rectangular baking dish with butter. Spread ½ of the Mexican/enchilada sauce in the bottom of the dish.
2. In a small bowl, combine all vegetables and ½ cup of the cheese.
3. Divide the bean mixture between tortillas and spread evenly over each one. Roll up and place seam-side down in the baking dish. Pour the rest of the enchilada sauce over the top and sprinkle with remaining ½ cup of cheese. Cover with foil.
4. Bake in a 200°C oven for about 15 minutes, or until heated through.
5. Keep the dish covered with foil to prevent the cheese from getting too crispy on top.

## Seasoned Spaghetti Pasta

**60 g per person spaghetti pasta**
**½ packet of seasoning from a noodle packet**

1. Place water in a saucepan and bring to boil; add spaghetti and simmer until just soft.
2. Drain and stir through seasoning.

## Fried Rice

**2 cups rice**
**½ finely chopped onion**
**¼ cup peas**
**¼ cup carrots, finely chopped**
**2 tbs oil**
**½ sachet of seasoning from a noodle packet**

1. Boil rice until soft, and drain. (Leave to sit in the fridge for an hour or more if you have time)
2. Heat 1 tbs oil in a frypan, add onion and cook until tender. Add peas and carrots and cook over low heat, stirring until well mixed.
3. Add 1 tbs oil to the frypan with seasoning and rice, continue stirring over low heat until well mixed and heated through.

**VARIATION - IF AVAILABLE FUNDS**

Add 1 large egg, if available. Move vegies over to one side of the pan, crack the egg into the opposite side and scramble until cooked and mix through the rice.

## Bircher Muesli

**1 cup water**
**1 cup milk**
**2 cups oats**
**1 apple, grated**
**¼ cup desiccated coconut**
**250 g vanilla yoghurt**

1. Put water, milk and oats in a saucepan and bring to boil, then simmer, stirring, until just tender – about 10 mins.

*Vegetarian Enchiladas* (Image © Sergu Koval)

Frugal Food | 37

2. Remove from heat and let cool, stirring, for about 10 mins. Add grated apple, coconut and yoghurt.

## Apple and Jam Rolls

**3 sheets of frozen pastry**
**your favourite jam**
**1-2 apples, sliced thinly or diced**
**desiccated coconut**

1. Cut each sheet of pastry into 6 pieces – total of 18 pieces.
2. Arrange the pieces on a greased baking tray.
3. Spread each piece with jam, add some apple, and sprinkle with coconut.
4. Roll diagonally from the corner.
5. Bake in a moderate oven until golden brown.

NB: These can also be made without the apple if you wish.

## Anzac Biscuits

**1 cup rolled oats**
**¾ cup desiccated coconut**
**1 cup plain flour, sifted**
**1 cup sugar**
**125 g butter, melted**
**2 tbs golden syrup**
**½ tsp bicarbonate of soda**
**3 tbs boiling water**

1. Place the oats, coconut, flour and sugar in a bowl. Stir to combine.
2. Melt the butter and golden syrup in a saucepan over low heat.
3. In a separate bowl, combine the bicarb soda and boiling water, then add this to the butter/syrup mixture.
4. Pour this (foaming) mixture into your dry mix and stir.
5. When well combined, roll into golf ball-sized balls, drop onto a tray spacing them about 6cm apart, and flatten a little with hand.
6. Bake for 15-18 minutes or until golden brown.

## Creamed Rice

**¾ cup uncooked white medium-grain rice**
**2 cups milk**
**½ tsp vanilla essence**
**⅓ cup sugar**
**1-2 cups water**

1. Boil rice as per packet until just soft.
2. Combine milk, vanilla and sugar in a medium saucepan, stirring over medium heat until sugar dissolves.
3. Turn down to a low simmer and add cooked rice. Cook partially covered over low heat, stirring occasionally, for 40 minutes or until rice is tender and creamy, adding more water as needed. Serve warm or cold, and with fruit if desired.

## Pancakes/Pikelets

**2 cups flour**
**1 tsp sugar**
**2 eggs, lightly beaten**
**1 cup milk**
**½-1 cup water**
**50 g butter, melted**

1. In a bowl, whisk flour and sugar.
2. Beat in the egg and then milk, a little at a time until batter is smooth and lump-free.
3. Melt a little butter in a hot pan over medium heat and pour in batter to cover the base.
4. When bubbles form on the surface, flip the pancake over and cook until lightly golden on the other side.

NB: For pikelets just make smaller pancakes, about the size of a tumbler glass bottom.

# Index

## Symbols

4-Egg Ham and Corn Quiche  17

## A

Anzac Biscuits  21, 29, 38
Apple and Jam Rolls  20, 28, 38
Apple Cake  12
Apple Crumble  12

## B

Basic Biscuit Dough  12
BBQ Sausages  26
Beef and Lentil Pasta  11
Bircher Muesli  37
Burgers and Meatballs  17

## C

Cheesy Veg Pie  36
Chilli Con Carne  17
Chilli Con Carne Nachos  20
Coconut and Oat Biscuits  13
Corn Fritters and Tomato Salsa  11
Country Chicken and Veg Pie  17
Creamed Rice  21, 29, 38
Creamy Coconut Vegetable Korma  33
Custard  12, 21, 28

## E

Easy Mayonnaise  13
Easy Vegetarian Pie  36
Echidnas  10

## F

Fish Cakes  27
Fried Rice  20, 26, 37

## H

Hummus  13

## L

Lentil and Vegie Patties  9
Lettuce Tuna Wraps  25

## M

Mince, Lentil and Spinach Curry  10

## N

Nachos  20, 34

## O

Onion and Cheese Sauce  9
Oven-Baked Chilli, Corn and Ham Fritters  27
Oven-Baked Chilli Corn Fritters  33

## P

Pancakes/Pikelets  7, 21, 29, 38
Pasta with Ham and Cheese Sauce  19
Pita Pizzas  18, 34
Porridge  7

## Q

Quick Quiche  8

## R

Rice and Vegie Pie  9
Rice Rissoles  35

## S

Satay or Butter Chicken and Rice  17
Satay Sausages and Rice  28
Sausage and Veg Parcels  26
Savoury Mince and Couscous  19
Seasoned Spaghetti Pasta  20, 28, 37
Shepherd's Pie  18
Slow Cooked Chicken  4, 7
Slow Cooked Chicken and Rice  7
Smoked Salmon Quiche  28
Spaghetti and Meatballs  17
Special Fried Rice (with Egg)  26
Spinach and Ricotta Cannelloni  8
Spring Pasta with Ham  26
Stir Fried Mince and Rice  9
Stir Fry Chicken and Noodles  19
Stuffed Oven-Baked Potatoes  18, 33

## T

Tacos and Burritos  25
Tasty Homemade Meat Pie  25
TexMex Rice  9
Traditional Lasagne  27
Tuna Mornay and Rice  19

## V

Vegetarian Chilli  33
Vegetarian Enchiladas  36
Vegetarian Lasagne  25, 34
Vegetarian Shepherd's Pie  34
Vegetarian Spaghetti  35
Vegie Fried Rice  11

## Z

Zucchini and Carrot Savoury Slice  10
Zucchini and Chicken Slice  7

www.ingramcontent.com/pod-product-compliance
Lightning Source LLC
Chambersburg PA
CBHW061800290426
44109CB00030B/2909